Second Edition
Cambridge Little Steps 1

Activity Book
Gabriela Zapiain

Contents

1. What can we see at school? — 3
2. What do we look like? — 17
3. What can our bodies do? — 31
4. What is a family? — 45
5. What is a pet? — 59
6. What do we eat? — 73
7. What is a toy? — 87
8. What can we see in a park? — 101
9. Where do we live? — 115

Picture Dictionary — 129

Stickers

 # What can we see at school?

 Point. Stick.  Color. Say.

Vocabulary: *teacher, boy, girl, school.* Say each new word, and children point to each item as you say it. Say: *(Girl / Boy)*. *Stick the (girl / boy).* Children stick each sticker as you say it. Then say: *(Teacher / School). Color the teacher / school.* Children color each item as you say it. Finally, children point to and name each item.

Circle. Say. — Story

Language: *What can you see? I can see a (tree). teacher, boy, girl, apple, bee, tree.* Ask children to remember the story. Children look at the pictures on the right. Point to each one and ask: *Is this from the story?* Children circle the pictures that appear in the story (they don't circle the picture of the kite). Point to each picture that appears in the story in turn and ask: *What can you see?* Children answer: *I can see a (tree).*

Unit 1

 Point. Say. Match. Follow.

Phonics

b

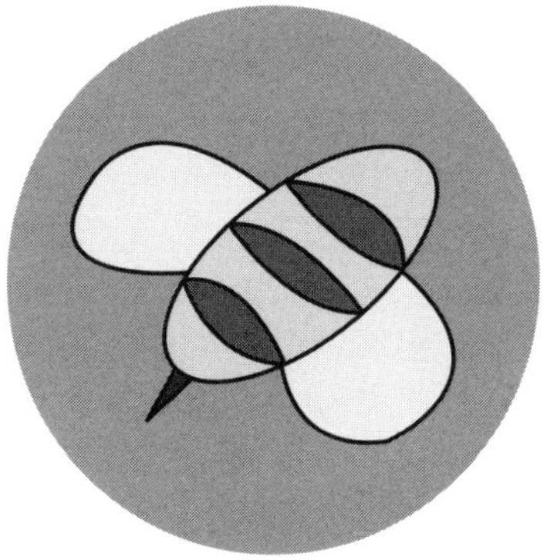

s

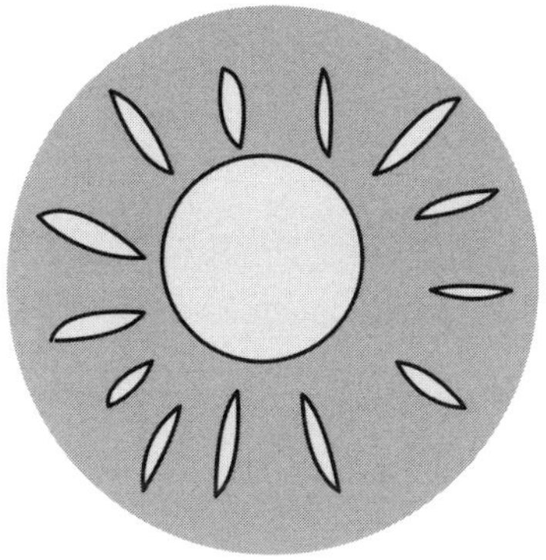

t

Phonics: *b*ee /b/, *s*un /s/, *t*ree /t/. Say the letter sounds /b/, /s/, /t/. Children point to the correct letter and repeat the sounds. Repeat with the words and pictures (*bee*, *sun*, *tree*). Next, say the letter sounds for children to point to the correct picture, or say the words and children point to the correct letter. Children trace the lines to match the letters to the pictures, and say the words. Finally, they follow the letters with their finger to help develop pre-writing skills.

Unit 1 5

 Say. Circle.

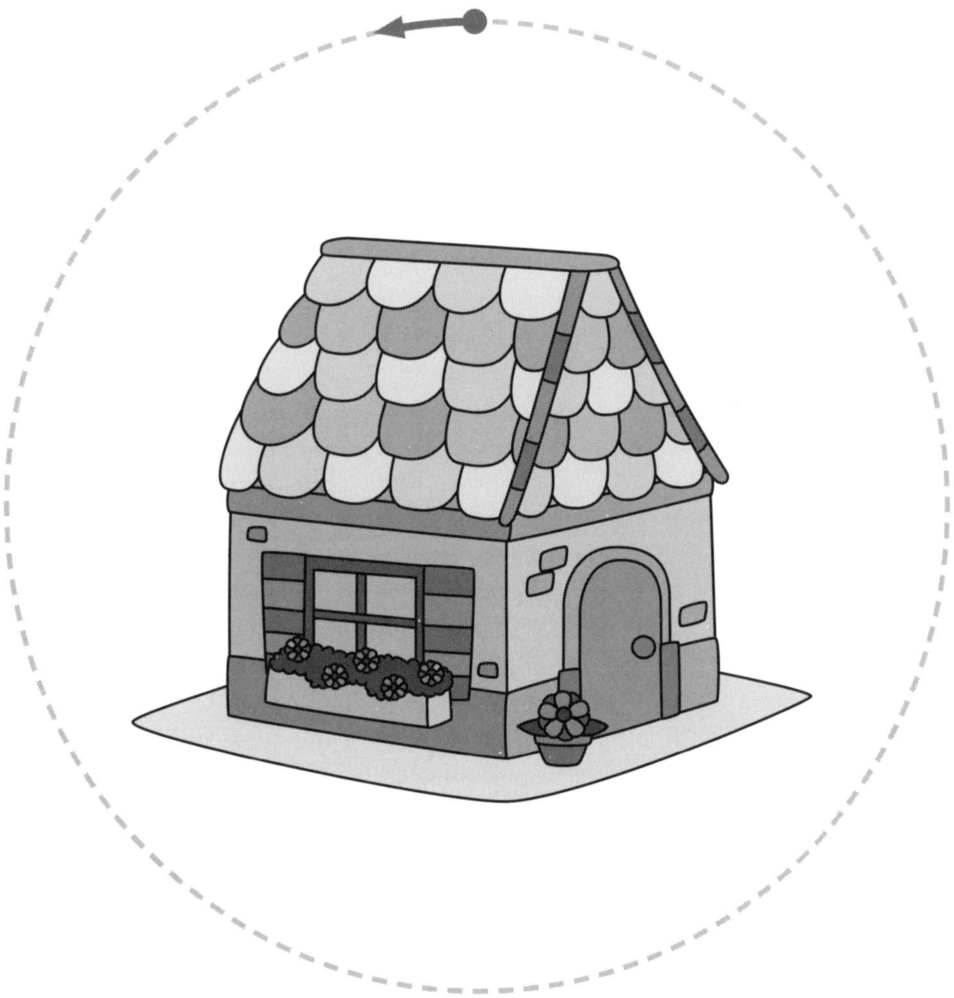

Literacy

Literacy: Identifying the setting for a story. Ask: *Where does the story take place?* Elicit answers and rephrase: *Yes, in a school.* Children circle the picture that shows where the story takes place (*school*).

👁 **Look.** 😊 **Say.** ✏️ **Color.**

Values

Values: Keeping the classroom clean. Look at the scene and ask: *Where are the children? (A classroom.)* Point to each child in the scene and ask: *What's he / she doing? Is he / she keeping the classroom clean? (Yes / No.)* If the answer is *No*, discuss why not and what they could do better. Finally, children identify and color the children who are keeping the classroom clean.

Unit 1 7

 Look.  Point.  Circle.  Say.

Vocabulary

   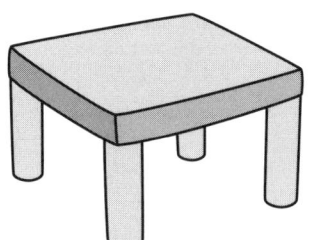

  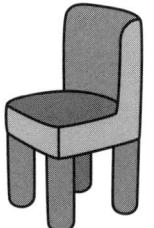 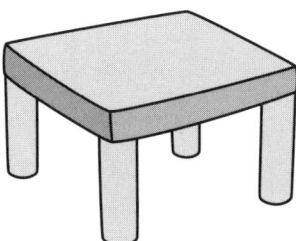

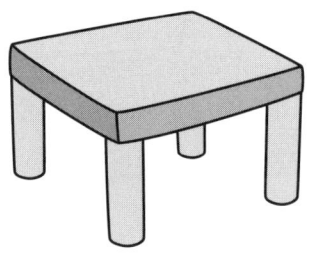 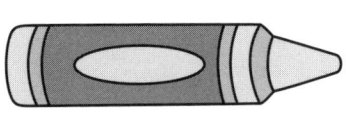  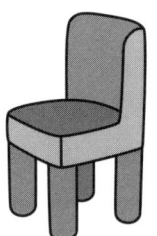

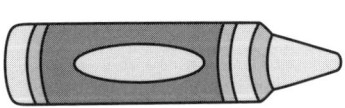  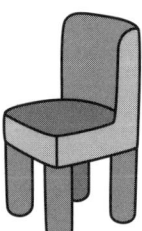 

Vocabulary: *book, crayon, chair, table.* Ask: *What can you see?* Point to each item in section 1, and say: *Book?* Highlight that the crayon is different, and children point to it. Children identify and point to the different item in each section. They can circle the items if they are able to. They then point to and name each item.

👁 Look. ✏️ Color. 😊 Say.

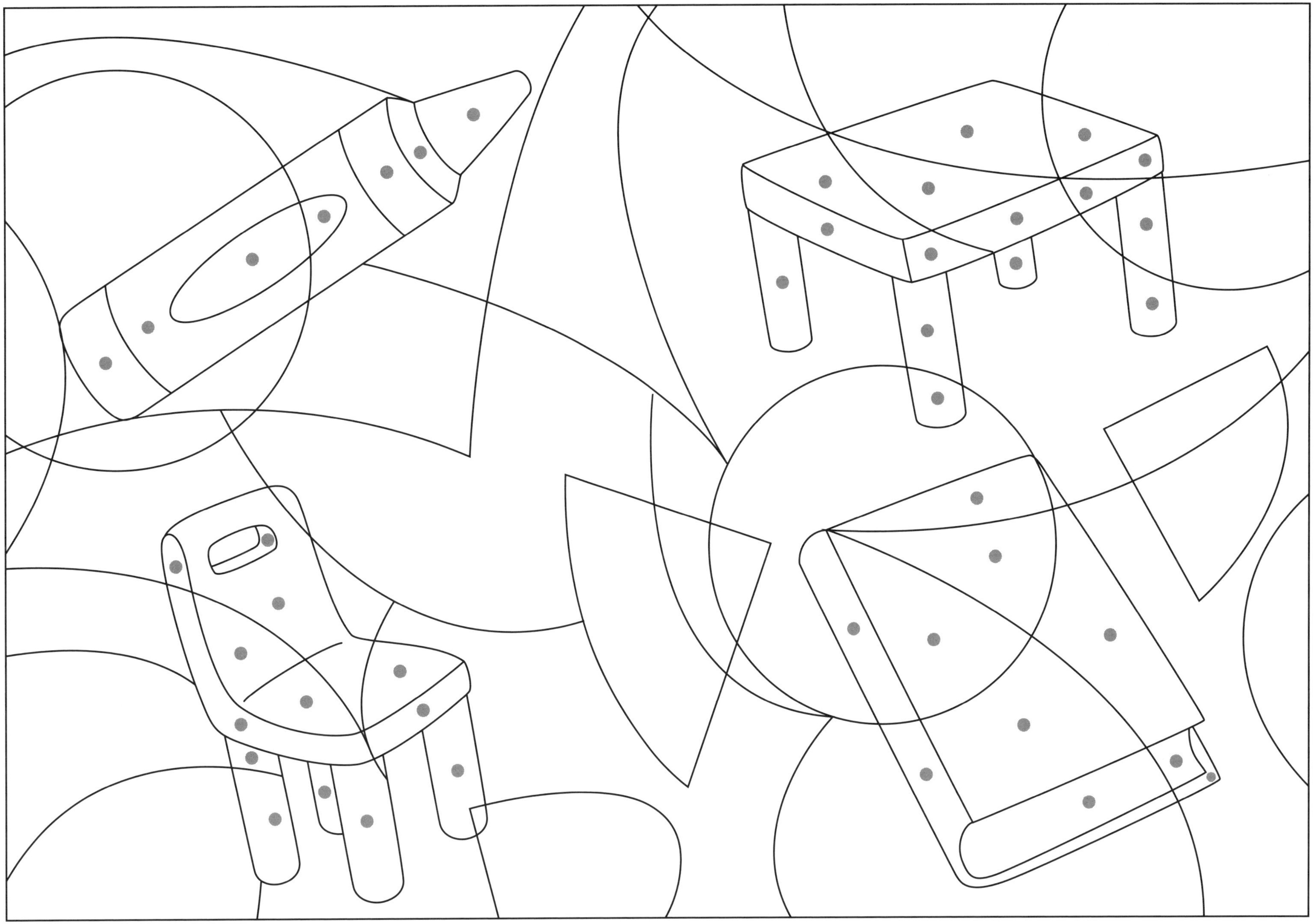

Language

Language: *Is it a (book)? Yes, it is. No, it isn't. What is it? It's a (crayon).* **Point to each picture and ask:** *What is it? Is it a (book)?* **Children guess what it might be. Then, they color every section with a dot in it to reveal each picture. As they do so, ask again:** *What is it?* **When children reveal each picture, they point and say:** *It's a (crayon)!*

👁 Look. ✏ Color. ◯ Circle. 😊 Say.

Concept

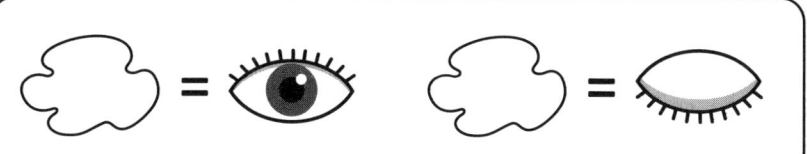

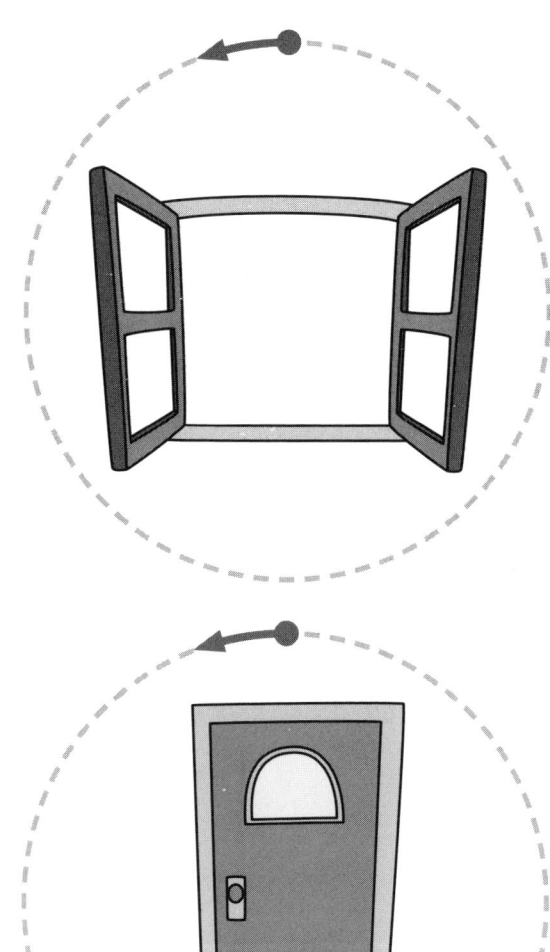
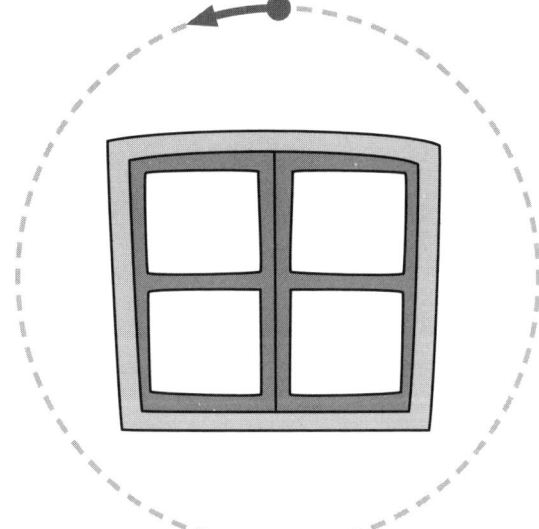

10 Unit 1

Concept: *open / closed*. Children choose two colors to represent *open* and *closed*, and complete the key at the top of the page. They then circle each picture in the correct color, according to their key. They point to each item and describe it: *The (book) is open. The (book) is closed.*

 Look.  Match. Say.

Vocabulary

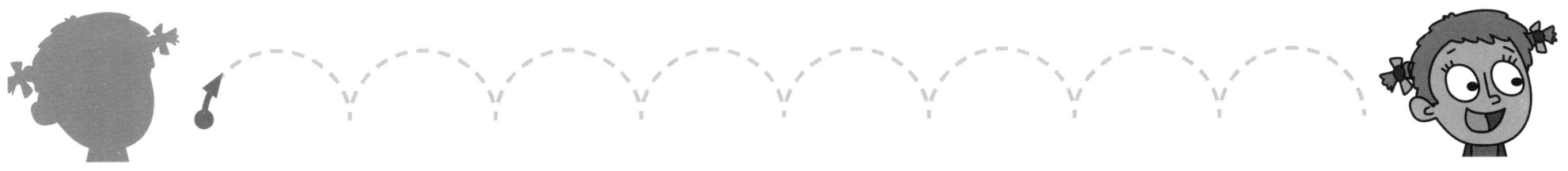

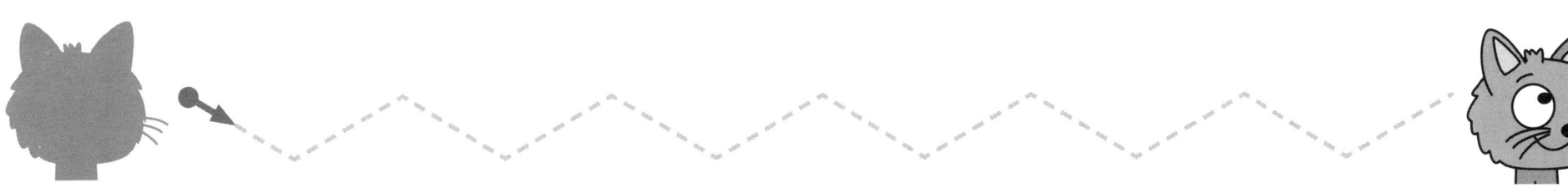

Vocabulary: *Leo, Tickles, Dad, Mia, Mom.* Point to each character in the second column and ask: *Who's this?* Children point along with you as you name the characters. Then, they trace the lines to match the silhouettes to the characters. Finally, children point to each character or silhouette and say the name.

👁 **Look.** ✏ **Draw.** 😊 **Say.**

Language

Language: *What's his / her name? His / Her name is (Mia). What's your name? My name is ...* Point to Leo and Mia and ask in turn: *What's his / her name?* Children answer. Then point to the blank head and explain that children should draw hair and color it to make the character look like themselves. As they work, ask each child: *What's your name?* and encourage them to answer: *My name is ...*

 Point. Match. Say. Speaking

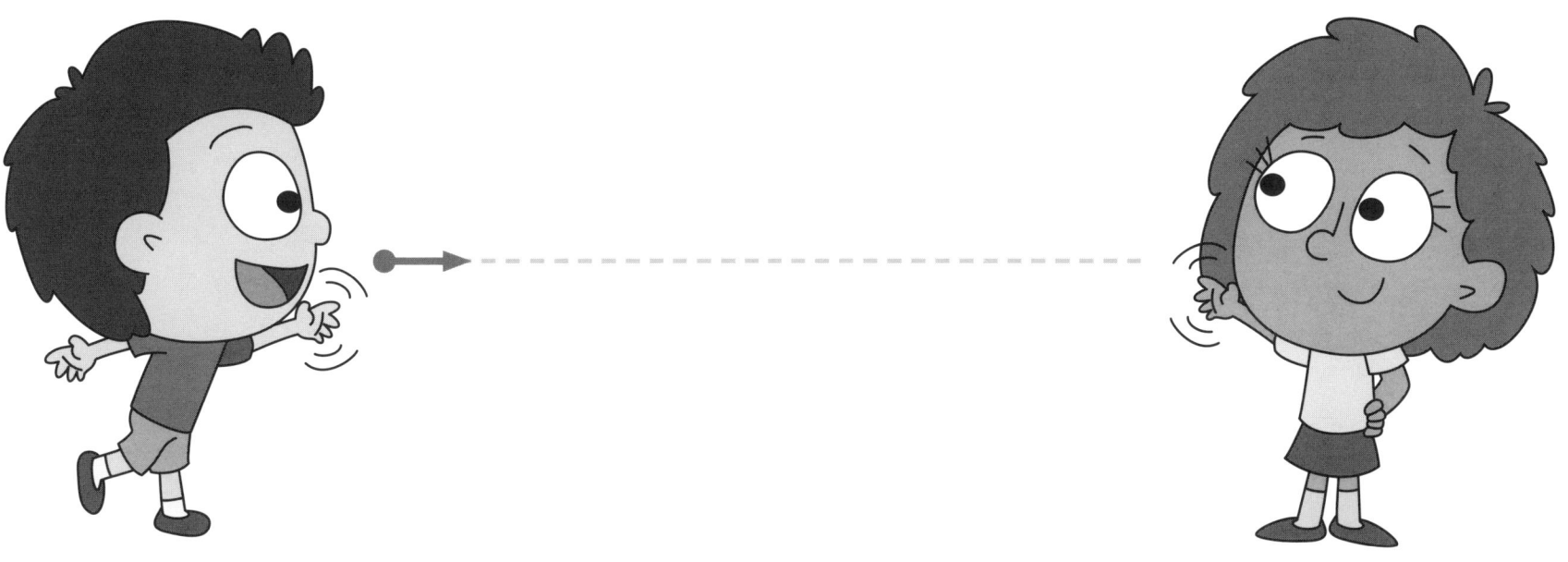

Language: *Hello! Hi! Goodbye! Bye-bye!* Children point to the pictures and decide whether the characters are saying *Hello* or *Goodbye* to each other. Then, they match the children saying *Hello*, and those saying *Goodbye*. Finally, children also say *Hello!* and *Goodbye!* to each other and mime the actions. Remind them they can say *Hi!* or *Bye-bye!* as alternatives.

👁 Look. 👆 Point. ⭕ Circle. 😃 Say.

Cross-curricular: Social Studies

Unit 1

Social Studies: Understanding the importance of classroom rules. Children look at the pictures. They point to the children who are following the class rules. They can circle the children if they are able to. Discuss the class rules by inviting children to point and repeat them as you name them: *Listen. Take turns. Share.*

Say. Trace. Count. Color.

Numeracy

Numeracy: one. Children say the *Number 1* Chant as they show one finger: *One, one, show me one. Show me one like this.* Then, they trace the number 1. Ask: *How many (books) can you see? Let's count. One (book).* Help children to count and choose one crayon, and use it to color the pictures.

Unit 1 15

Say. Circle. Draw. Color.

Review

What can we see at school?

My favorite thing in Unit 1:

Unit 1

Vocabulary and Language Review: Ask the Big Question: *What can we see at school?* Children look back through Unit 1 to recall what they have learned. Ask children to look at the six pictures from Unit 1. They say the words then circle the pictures that they are able to name. Then ask: *What was your favorite thing in this unit?* Remind children of the song, story, cross-curricular lesson, etc. They draw a picture of their favorite thing. Children point to and talk about their pictures. Answer the Big Question together, using their pictures as a prompt. Finally, focus on the self-assessment activity. Ask: *How did you do in this unit?* Children color the face that shows how they feel they did.

 # What do we look like?

 Point. Stick. Color.  Say.

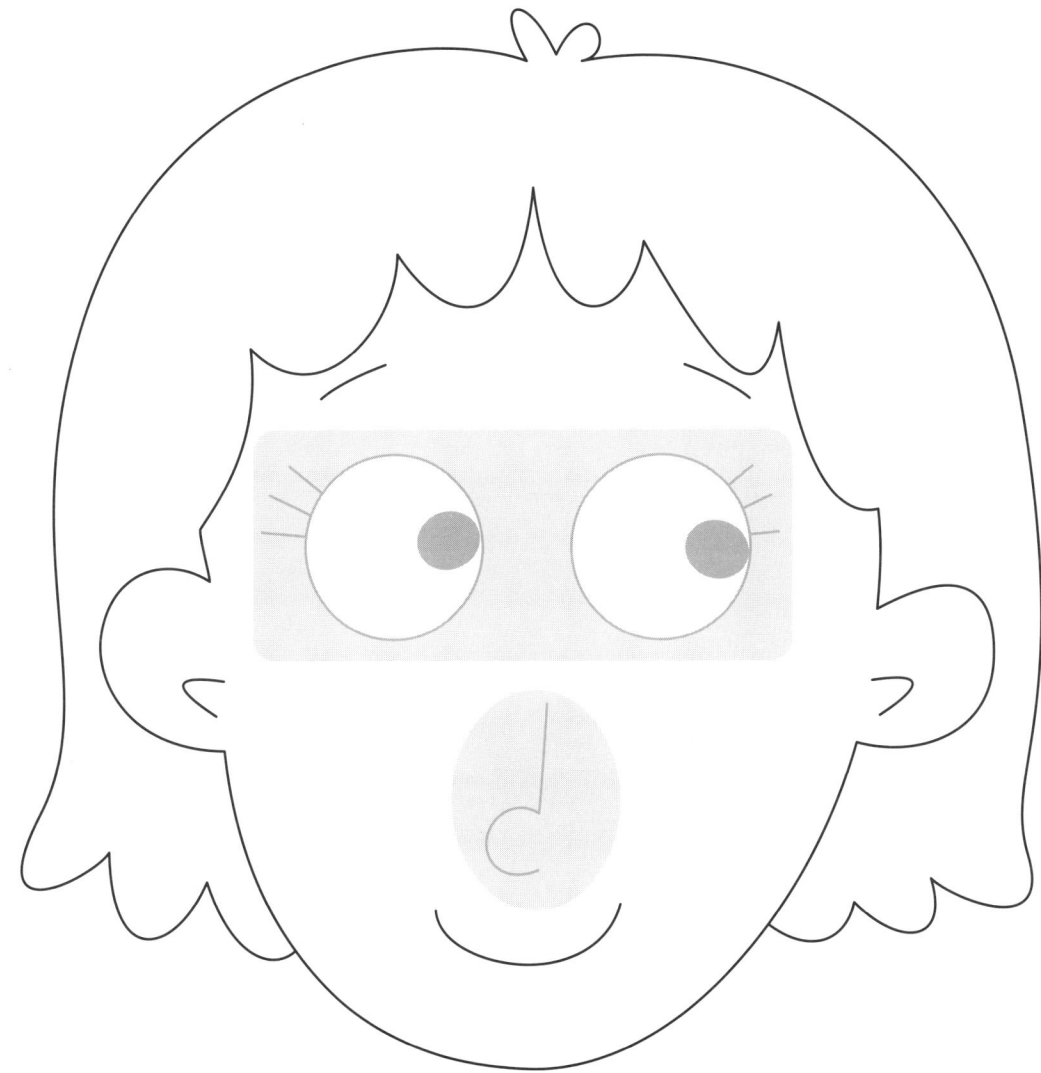

Vocabulary: *face, hair, eyes, nose.* Say each new word, and children point to each feature as you say it. Say: *(Eyes / Nose). Stick the (eyes / nose).* Children stick each sticker as you say it. Then say: *(Face / Hair). Color the face / hair.* Children color each feature as you say it. Finally, children point to and name each feature.

 Point.  Match. Say. Story

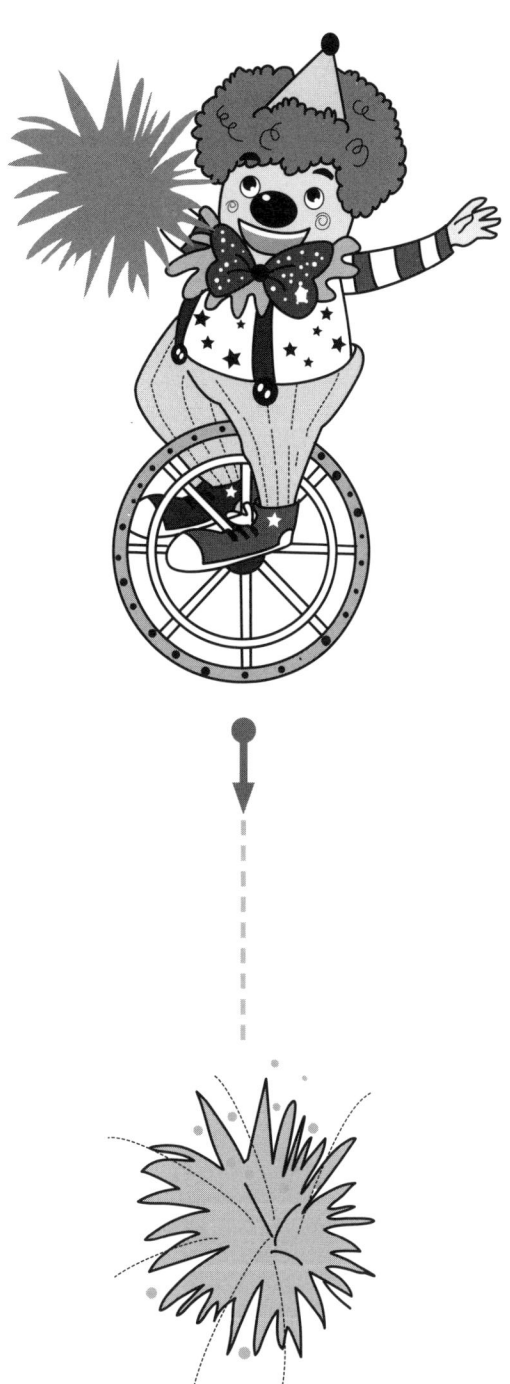
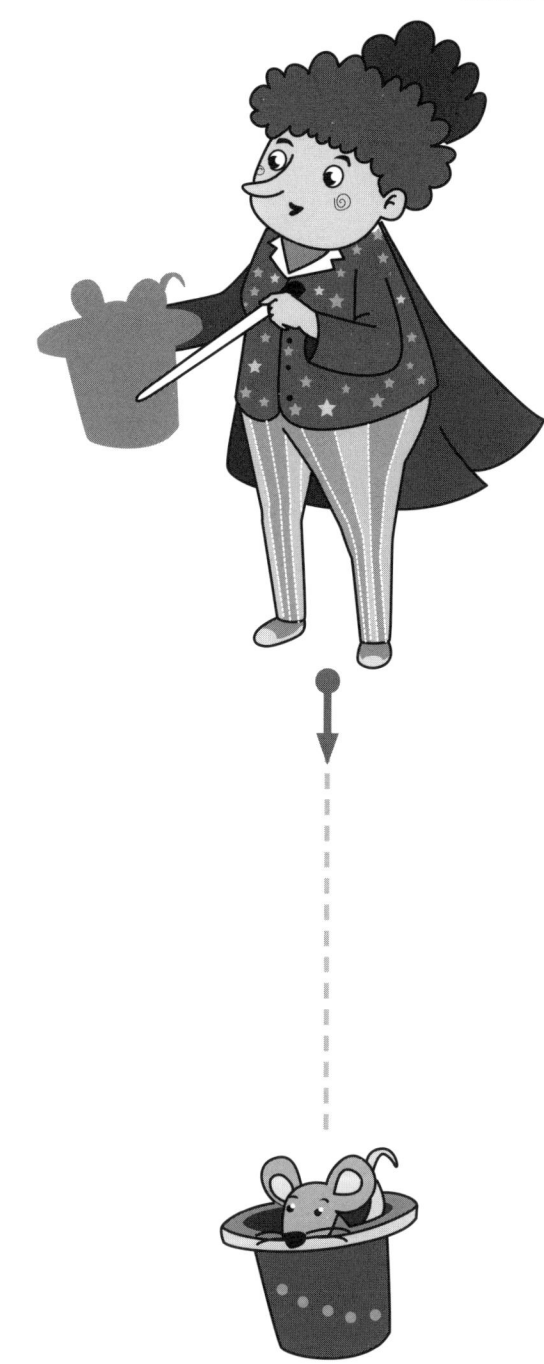
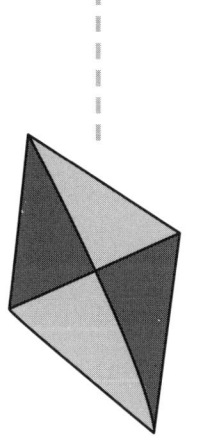

Language: *Can you find me? I have a (kite). hat, kite, mop, mouse.* Say: *Can you find me? I have a kite.* Children point to the boy holding the silhouette of the kite. They match the boy to the kite. Repeat for the other two pictures. When children have finished, point to each character in turn. Say: *I have a kite / a mop / a mouse in a hat.* Children repeat after you.

👆 Point. 👄 Say. 🔄 Circle. ➡ Follow.

Phonics

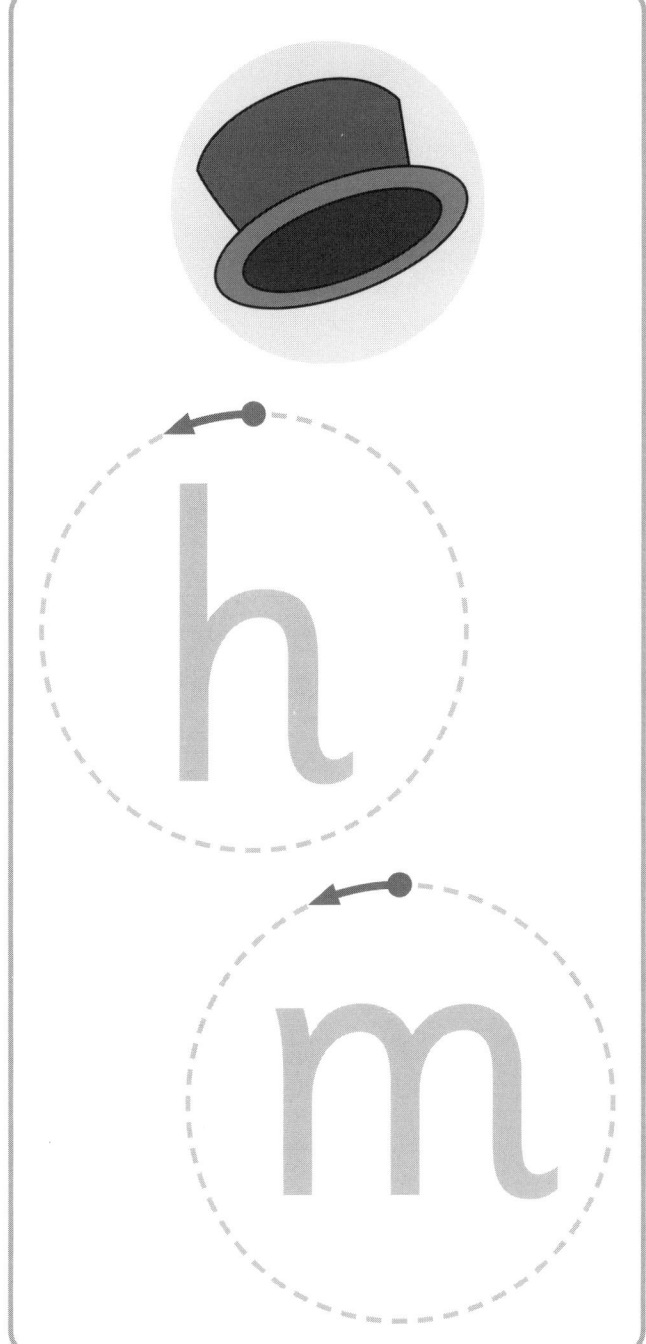
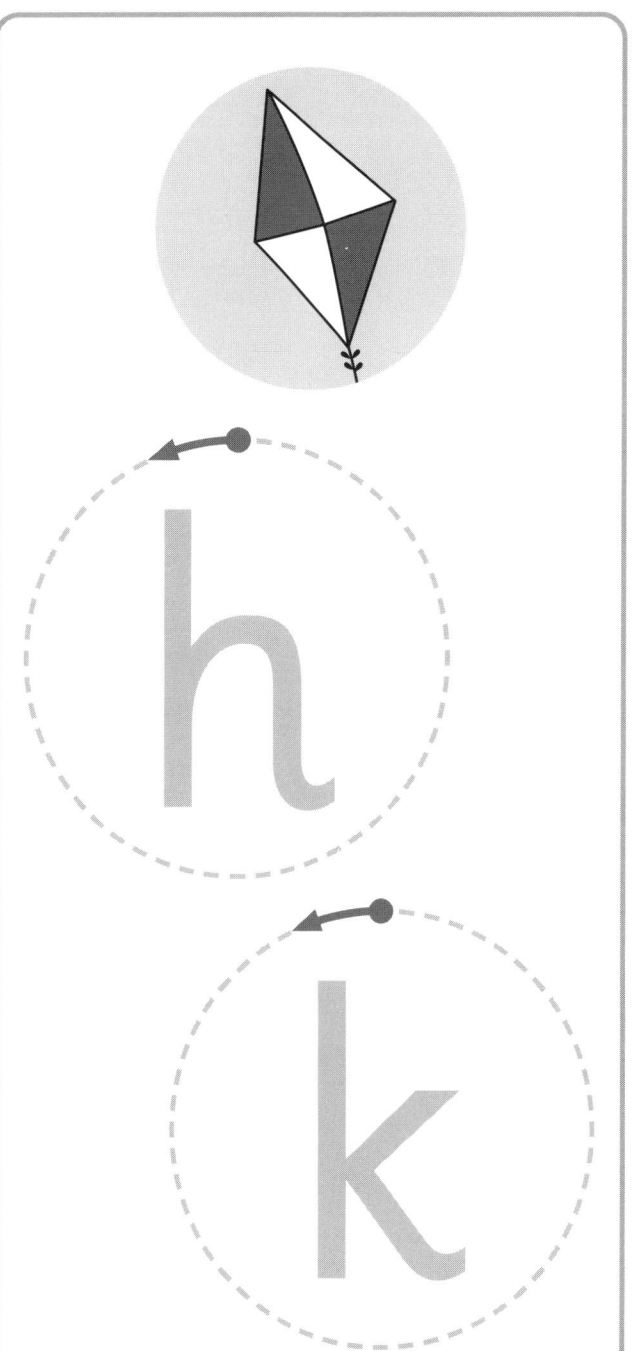
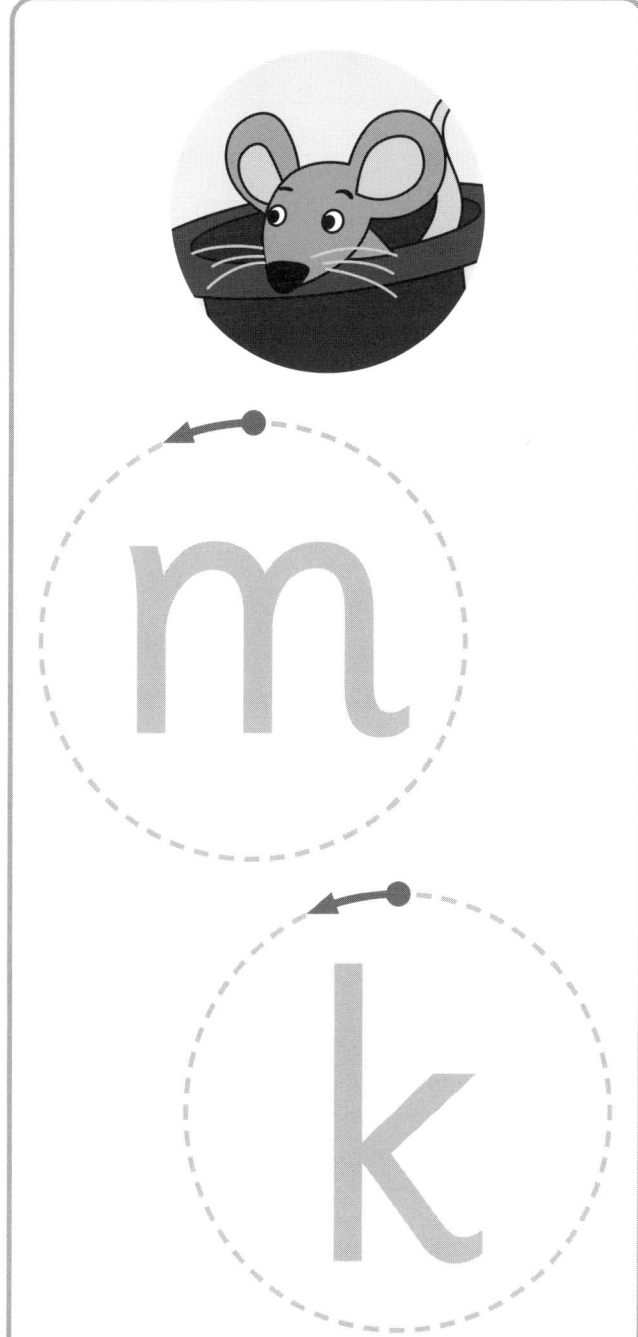

Phonics: *h*at /h/, *k*ite /k/, *m*ouse /m/. Say the words in turn. Children point to the correct picture. Next, say the letter sounds /h/, /k/, /m/ for children to point to the correct letter and repeat the sounds. Children trace the circles to identify the correct letter for each picture, and say the words. Finally, they follow the letters with their finger to help develop pre-writing skills.

Unit 2

 Say. Circle. Color.

Literacy

Literacy: Identifying characters from a story. Children look at the pictures of characters. Point to each one and ask: *Is this a character from the story?* Children answer: *Yes* or *No*. Children circle the characters who appear in the story. Then point to the first character and ask: *What color is his hair?* Children color the characters' hair to match the story.

Unit 2

 Look. Choose. Draw. Color.

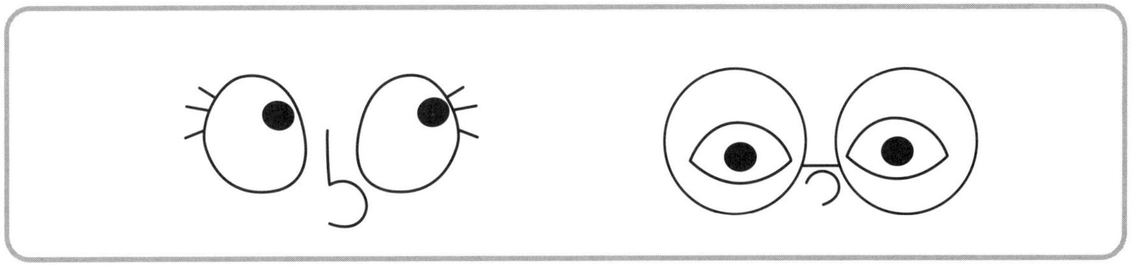

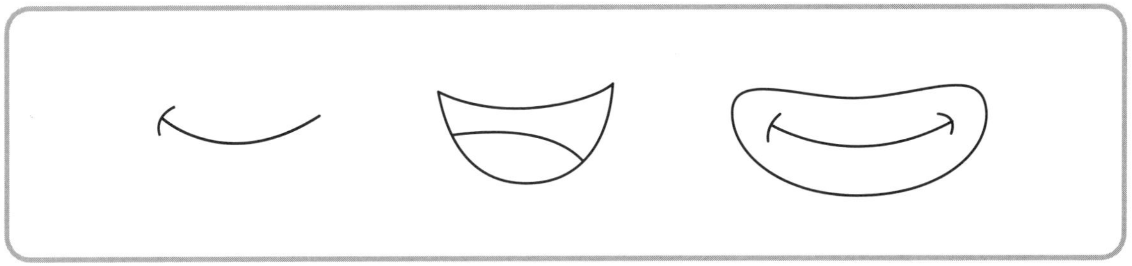

Values

Values: Celebrating differences. Explain that children are going to invent a character. They look at each set of pictures. They choose hair, eyes, a mouth, and an outfit for their character, and draw and color them on the character's outline. When they have finished, invite children to show their characters to you and the class. Discuss how the characters are the same and how they are different. Remind children that we are all different and that makes us all special!

Unit 2 21

 Point.  Trace.  Color.  Say.

Vocabulary

Vocabulary: *forehead, ears, cheeks, mouth.* Ask: *What can you see?* Name the facial features in turn, and children point to each one as you name it. Say: *Trace the (forehead).* Children trace the features, then color them. They then point to and name each feature.

Look. Match. Say.

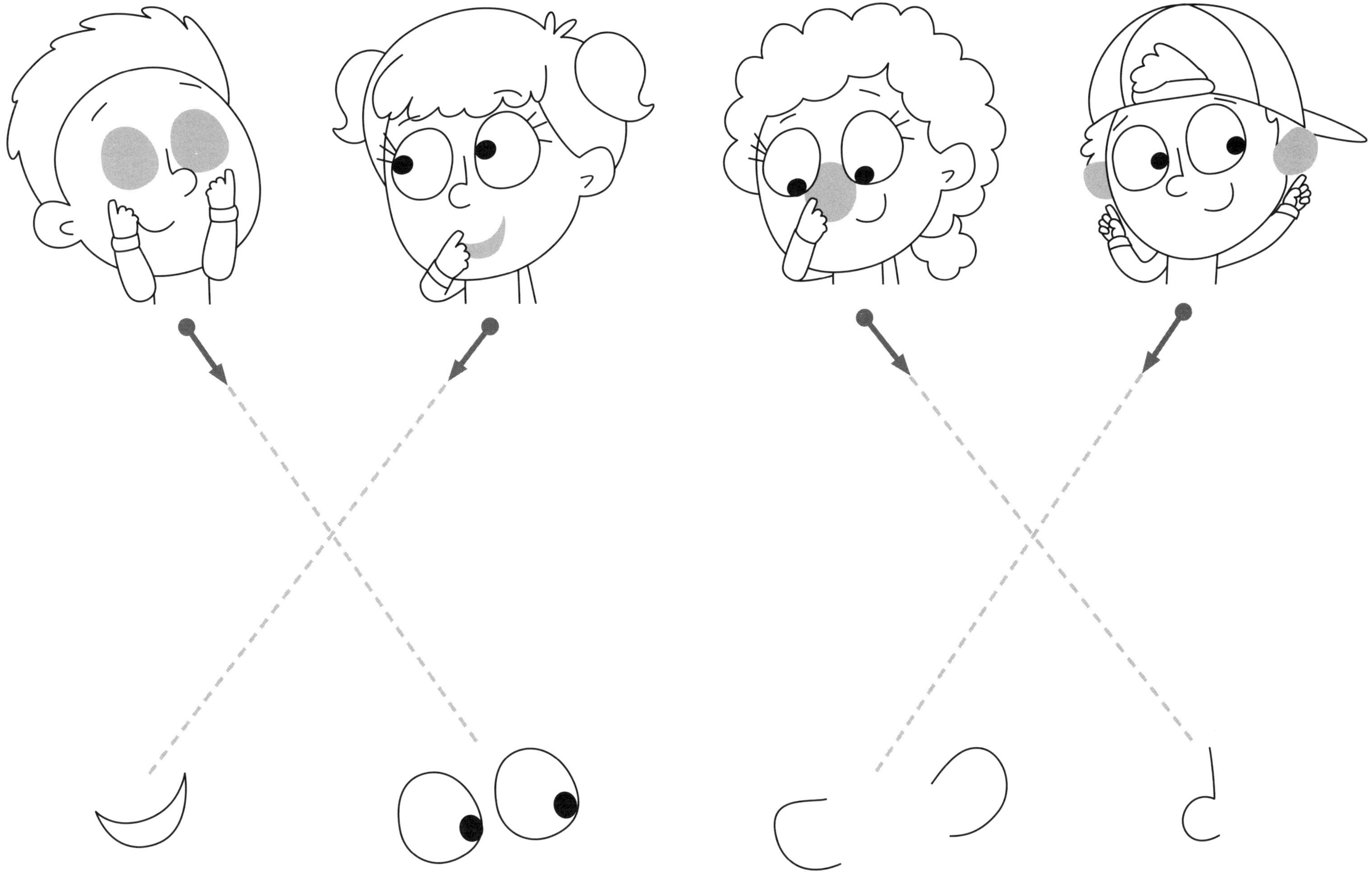

Language

Language: *This is my (mouth). These are my (eyes).* Children look at the pictures and name the missing facial features: *eyes, mouth, nose, ears.* Then, they match the faces to the missing facial features. Finally, children point to the features one at a time, name them, and point to the corresponding features on their own face. They say: *This is my (mouth). These are my (eyes).*

Unit 2 23

 Color. Match.

Concept

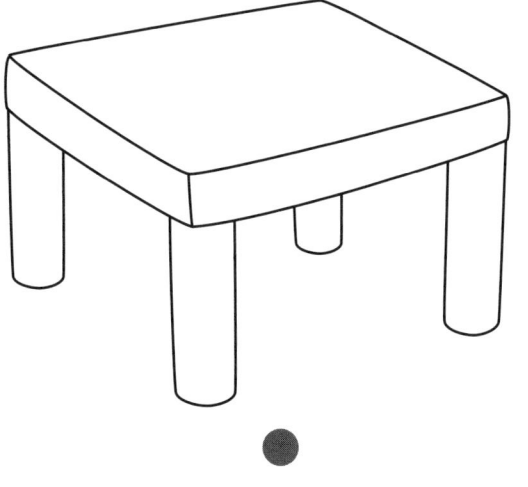
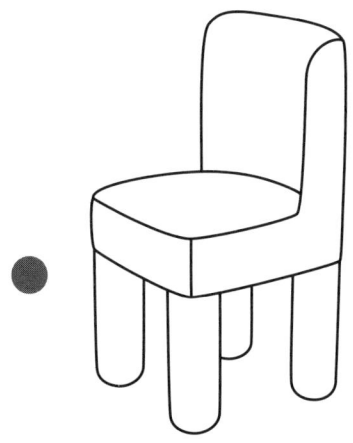
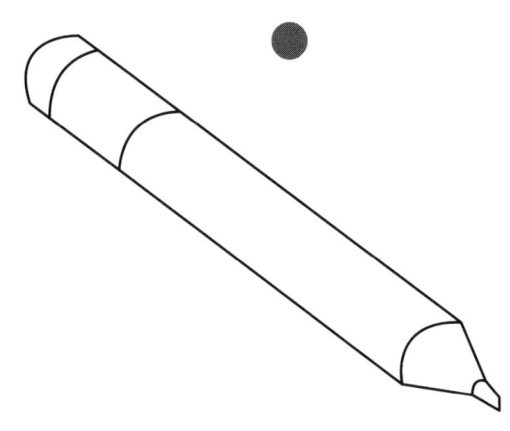

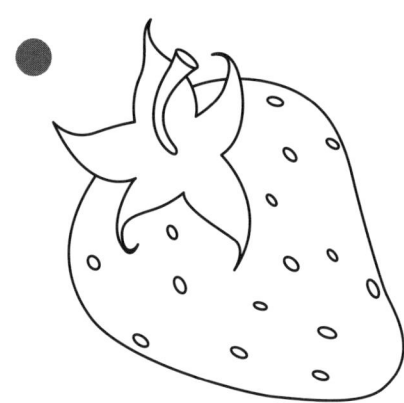

Concept: Categorizing by color. Distribute crayons. Point to the banana. Ask: *What color is it?* Children color the banana yellow. Point to the table. Ask: *What color is your table?* Children color the table. Repeat with all the pictures. When children have finished coloring the objects, they draw lines to match objects of the same color.

👁 **Look.** ✏️ **Color.** 😊 **Say.**

Vocabulary

Vocabulary: happy, sad, angry. Children choose colors to represent *happy*, *sad*, and *angry*, and complete the key at the top of the page. They then color each face according to their key. Show them how to spin a crayon on the page, and see where it points. Ask: *How does he / she feel? (Angry. / Sad. / Happy.)* When children understand the game, they can play it in pairs or groups.

Unit 2 25

 Trace.  Say.  Circle.   Language

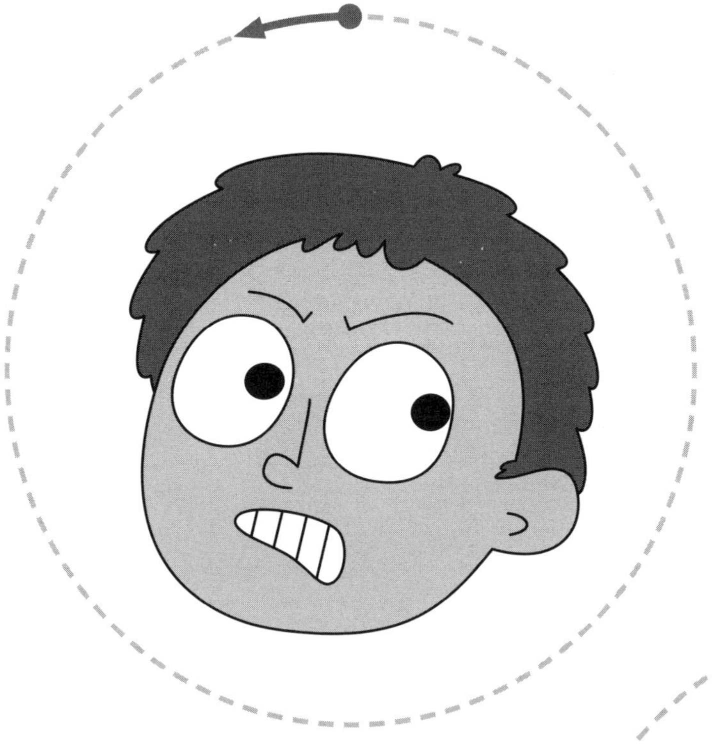

Language: *How do you feel? I feel (happy). Are you (sad)? Yes, I am. No, I'm not. Is he / she angry? Yes, he / she is. No, he / she isn't.* **Point to Mia and ask:** *How does she feel? (Happy.)* Repeat with the remaining characters. Then, children trace the happy and sad mouths. Ensure they are tracing left to right. When they're finished, point to each character and ask: *How do you feel today?* Children say how they feel, and circle the face that shows that emotion.

✏️ **Trace.** ✏️ **Draw.** 😊 **Say.**

Speaking

Language: *How do you feel? I feel (happy).* Point to each face and say: *Happy or sad?* eliciting the answers. Children trace the faces and the mouths. Ask them to draw hair and color the faces to look like themselves. You can use yarn or paint for the hair if you like. As they're working, go around pointing to the faces and asking: *How do you feel? (I feel happy / sad.)*

Look. Say. Color.

Cross-curricular: Science

Science: Recognizing similarities and differences in appearance. Say: *Look at the children.* Point to the first pair and say: *Do they look the same or different? What's different? What's the same?* Repeat with the other pictures. Ask if each of the pairs of children can be twins. Remind them some twins look the same and some look different. Children color the children who can be twins.

 Say.  Trace.  Count. Color.

Numeracy

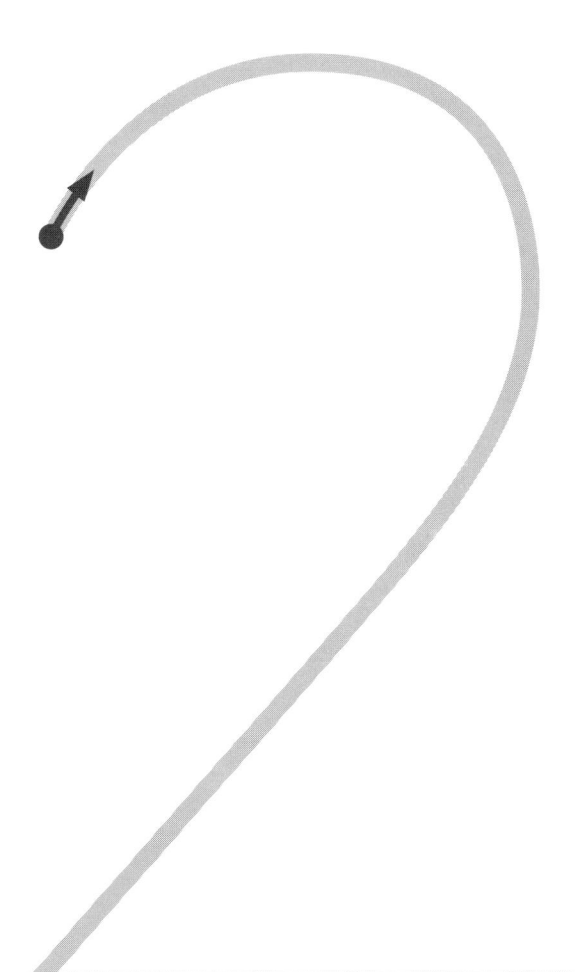

Numeracy: two. Children say the *Number 2* Chant as they show two fingers: *Two, two, show me two. Show me two like this.* Then, they trace the number 2. Ask: *How many eyes can you see? Let's count: One, two.* Repeat, encouraging children to count. Help children to count and choose two crayons and use them to color the picture. Finally, children count a partner's two eyes and two ears as they repeat: *one, two, one, two.*

Unit 2 · 29

 Say. Circle. Draw. Color.

Review

What do we look like?

My favorite thing in Unit 2:

Unit 2

Vocabulary and Language Review: Ask the Big Question: *What do we look like?* Children look back through Unit 2 to recall what they have learned. Ask them to look at the six pictures from Unit 2. They say the words and then circle the pictures that they are able to name. Then ask: *What was your favorite thing in this unit?* Remind children of the song, story, cross-curricular lesson, etc. They draw a picture of their favorite thing. Children point to and talk about their pictures. Answer the Big Question together, using their pictures as a prompt. Finally, focus on the self-assessment activity. Ask: *How did you do in this unit?* Children color the face that shows how they feel they did.

3 What can our bodies do?

 Point. Stick. Color. Say.

Vocabulary: *arms, hands, legs, feet.* Say each new word, and children point to each body part as you say it. Say: *(Hands / Feet)*. Stick the *(hands / feet)* on the *girl*. Children stick each sticker on the girl as you say it. Then say: *(Arms / Legs)*. *Color the arms / legs on the boy.* Children color each body part (on the boy only) as you say it. Finally, children point to and name each body part.

 Circle. Say.

Story

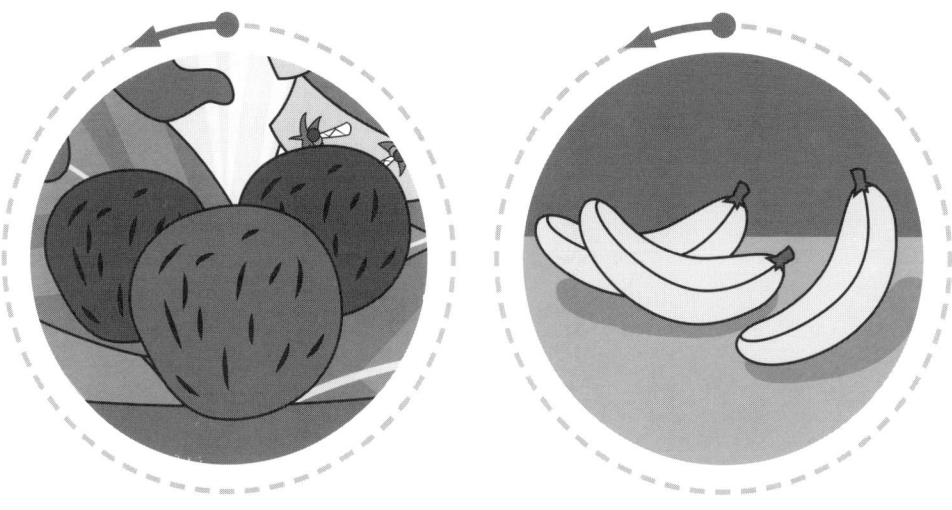

Language: *What can you see? I can see (coconuts). coconut, gorilla.* Children look at the big picture. Ask: *What can you see?* Children circle the picture in the top pair of pictures that shows the items in the big picture. They say: *I can see (coconuts).* Repeat with the bottom pair of pictures.

 Point. Say. Match. Follow.

Phonics

g

j

f

Phonics: *g*orilla /g/, *j*ump /dʒ/, *f*eet /f/. Say the letter sounds /g/, /dʒ/, /f/. Children point to the correct letter and repeat the sounds. Next, say the words for children to point to the correct picture. Children trace the lines to match the letters to the pictures, and say the words. Finally, children follow the letters with their finger to help develop pre-writing skills.

 Look. Circle. Color.

Literacy

Literacy: Identifying scenes from a story. Ask children to think about the story and remember the characters and what happens. Then focus on the pictures. Children look carefully, and identify and circle the five differences. Then ask: *Which picture is from the story?* Children color the circle of the correct picture.

Look. Say. Circle.

Values

Values: Washing our hands. Children look at the picture of the girl and describe what they see. Ask: *What is she doing? (Washing hands.)* Then point to the four pictures in the middle of the page. Ask: *What does she need to wash her hands?* Children circle the things that are needed to wash your hands.

👉 Point. ✨ Match. 😊 Say.

Vocabulary

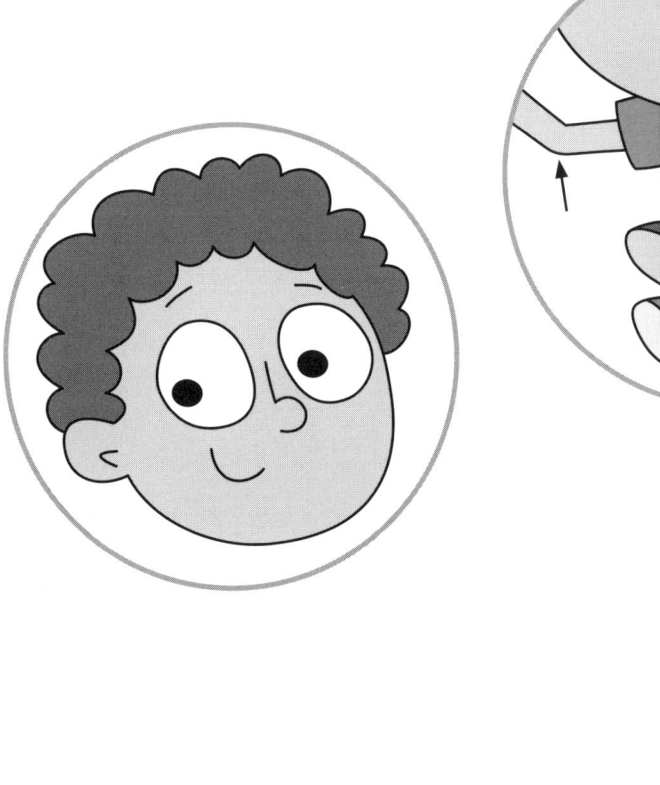
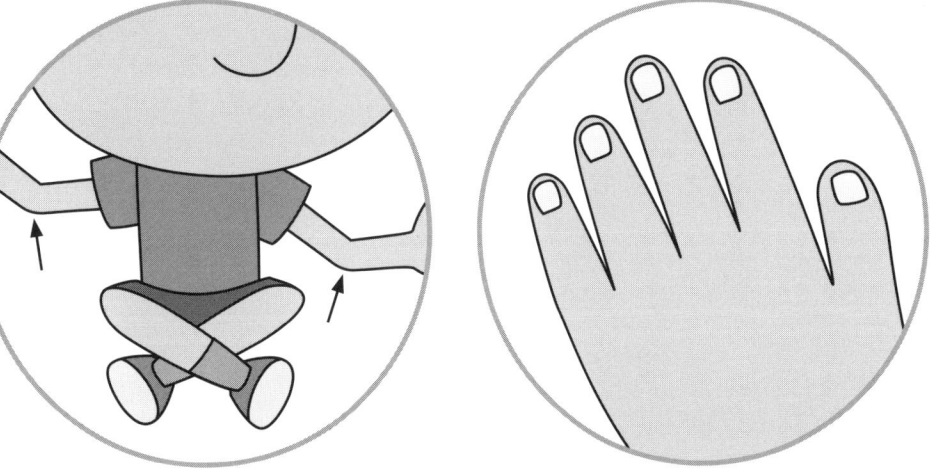
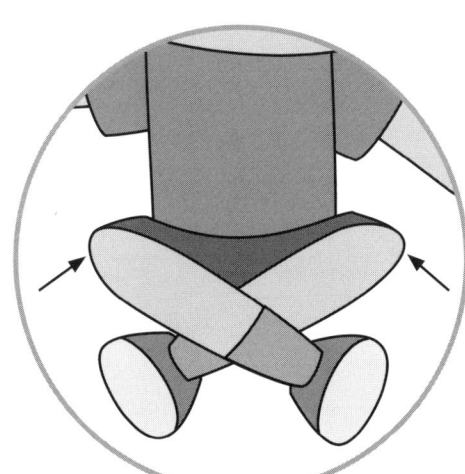

Vocabulary: *head, fingers, elbows, knees.* Children point to and name the body parts: *head, elbows, fingers, knees.* Then, they look at the boy at the bottom of the page and draw lines to match the body parts at the top of the page to the corresponding parts on the boy's body. Finally, finger trace each line, repeating the name of the body part as you link the pictures. Children say the name of each body part after you.

 Match. Say.

Language

Language: *How many (knees) does he / she have? He / She has (two knees).* Children look at the pictures at the top of the page and name the body parts shown in silhouette in each picture. They trace the lines to match each child to the appropriate body parts. They then point and say: *He / She has (two ears).*

Unit 3 | 37

Look. Color. Circle. Say.

Concept

Concept: *up / down*. Children choose two colors to represent *up* and *down*, and complete the key at the top of the page. They then circle each picture in the correct color, according to their key. They point to each picture and describe it: *His arm is up. His arm is down.*

 **Look.**  **Circle.**  **Say.**

Vocabulary

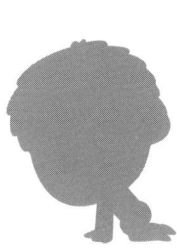   

Vocabulary: *run, dance, crawl, kick.* Children point to and name the actions in the dotted circles: *kick, dance, run, crawl.* Point to the silhouette on the top row, and ask children what action it represents *(Dance.).* They find and circle the picture that matches the silhouette. Ask: *Can you dance?* and encourage children to show you if they say *Yes.* Repeat with the other three rows.

Unit 3 39

 Match. Say.

Language

Language: *Can he / she (dance)? Yes, he / she can. No, he / she can't. He / She can (run).* Point to the first child and ask: *Can he run? Can he dance? Can he kick?* Repeat as you point to each action. Finger trace the line from the boy to the action, then say: *He can (dance)!* Children trace the lines. Then, with your help, they say each action: *He can dance. She can run. He can kick (a ball).*

Follow. Say.

Speaking

Language: *May I (wash my hands)? Yes, you may.* Remind children how we ask permission to go to the bathroom or wash our hands: *May I (wash my hands)?* Children repeat. Focus on the child on the left. Ask: *What does he say? (May I wash my hands?)* Say: *Yes, you may.* Children finger trace the path to the picture of the child washing his hands. They then trace it with a pencil. When they finish, they point and say: *I wash my hands!*

 Say. Make.

Cross-curricular: Art

My Fingerprints

Art: Learning how we can use our bodies to be creative. Say: *Show me your fingers*. Children hold up their fingers and wiggle them in the air. Ask: *What can you do with your fingers?* Elicit answers, including *We can paint*. Then say: *We can make fingerprints!* and explain what it means. Children press each finger of their left hand onto an inkpad. Then, they make fingerprints on the corresponding fingers of the left-hand outline. Monitor to ensure they make each fingerprint in the correct place. Repeat with the right hand.

 Say.  Trace.  Count. Color.

Numeracy

Numeracy: *three*. Children say the *Number 3* Chant as they show three fingers: *Three, three, show me three. Show me three like this.* Then, they trace the number 3. Ask: *How many children can you see? Let's count: One, two, three.* Repeat, encouraging children to count. Help children to count and choose three crayons and use them to color the pictures.

Say. Circle. Draw. Color.   Review

What can our bodies do?

My favorite thing in Unit 3:

Unit 3

Vocabulary and Language Review: Ask the Big Question: *What can our bodies do?* Children look back through Unit 3 to recall what they have learned. Ask them to look at the six pictures from Unit 3. They say the words and then circle the pictures that they are able to name. Then ask: *What was your favorite thing in this unit?* Remind children of the song, story, cross-curricular lesson, etc. They draw a picture of their favorite thing. Children point to and talk about their pictures. Answer the Big Question together, using their pictures as a prompt. Finally, focus on the self-assessment activity. Ask: *How did you do in this unit?* Children color the face that shows how they feel they did.

4 What is a family?

 Point. Stick. Color. Say.

Vocabulary: *father, mother, sister, brother.* Say each new word, and children point to each family member as you say it. Say: *(Mother / Father).* Stick the *(mother / father).* Children stick each sticker as you say it. Then say: *(Sister / Brother). Color the sister / brother.* Children color each family member as you say it. Finally, children point to and name each family member.

Unit 4　45

 Color. Say.

Story

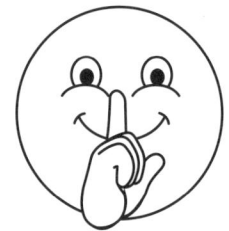 

Language: *Is it (noisy)? noisy, quiet.* Look at the first picture. Ask: *Is it noisy or quiet?* Children color the quiet or noisy emoji. Do the same for the second picture. When children have finished they describe each picture: *It's noisy / quiet.*

 **Point.**  **Say.**  **Match.** ➤ **Follow.**

Phonics

d

l

n

Phonics: *duck* /d/, *lamb* /l/, *night* /n/. Say the letter sounds /d/, /l/, /n/. Children point to the correct letter and repeat the sounds. Repeat with the words and pictures (*duck, lamb, night*). Next, say the letter sounds for children to point to the correct picture, or say the words and children point to the correct letter. Children trace the lines to match the letters to the pictures, and say the words. Finally, children follow the letters with their finger, or, if they are ready, they can trace them with a pencil.

Unit 4

 Say. Circle. Color.

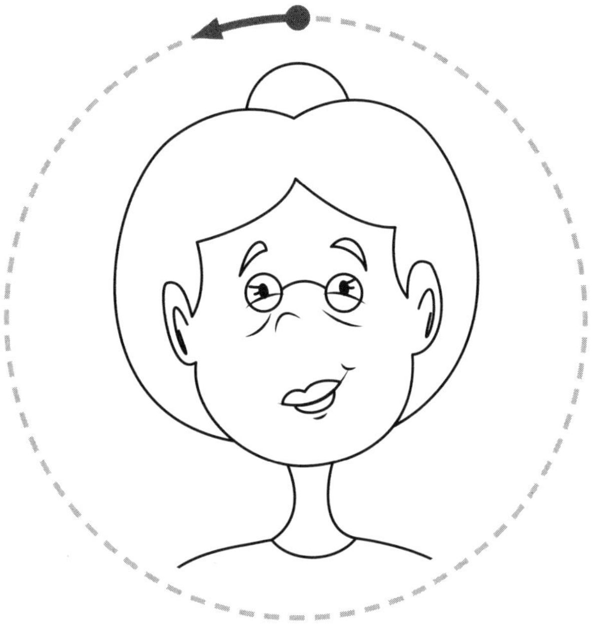

Literacy

Literacy: Identifying characters from a story. Children look at the pictures of characters. Ask: *Who's this? Who is in the story? (Father.)* Then point to each one and ask: *Is this a character from the story?* Children circle the characters who appear in the story. Then point to the first character and ask: *What color is his (hair)?* Children color the characters' hair and clothes to match the story.

Look. Say. Trace.

Values

Values: Appreciating our family. Children look at the pictures and say what they see. Ask them what the girl is doing in the first picture, and what help she needs. Ask them to find the picture that shows what happens next, and what happens after that. Children trace the lines to match the pictures.

Unit 4

 Say. Follow. — Vocabulary

Vocabulary: *mother, grandfather, grandmother, baby.* Point to the mother and ask children: *Who's this?* Demonstrate by finger tracing how to follow the path to the baby then point and say: *Baby* as children repeat. Do the same for *grandfather* and *grandmother*. Then explain that children should follow the paths between family members, drawing a path through each maze with a crayon and repeating their names.

 50 Unit 4

 **Look. Match. Say.**

Language

Language: *Is she the (grandmother)? Is he the (father)? Yes, he / she is. No, he / she isn't. This is the (mother).* Children look at the picture at the top of the page. Point to different people and ask: *Is (he) the (father)?* Children answer: *Yes, he / she is* or *No, he / she isn't*. Then, they look at the large picture, and draw lines to match the people to the silhouettes. They point to the small pictures and say: *This is the (sister).*

Unit 4 · 51

Look. Color. Say.

Concept: *adults / children.* Look at the scene and ask: *What can you see? (A family.)* Point to each person in the scene and ask: *Is he / she (an adult)?* Children choose two colors to represent *adult* and *child*, and complete the key at the top of the page. They then color each person in the correct color, according to their key. They point to each person and say: *He's / She's (an adult).*

Unit 4

👁 Look. 👆 Point. ⭕ Circle. 😃 Say.

Vocabulary

Vocabulary: *young, old, short, tall.* Ask: *What can you see?* Point to each person in section 1 and say: *Old? Young?* Highlight that the grandmother is different, because she is old, and children point to her. Children identify and point to the different person in each section. They can circle them if they are able to. They then point to each one and say: *He's / She's (tall).*

Unit 4 53

 Match. Say.

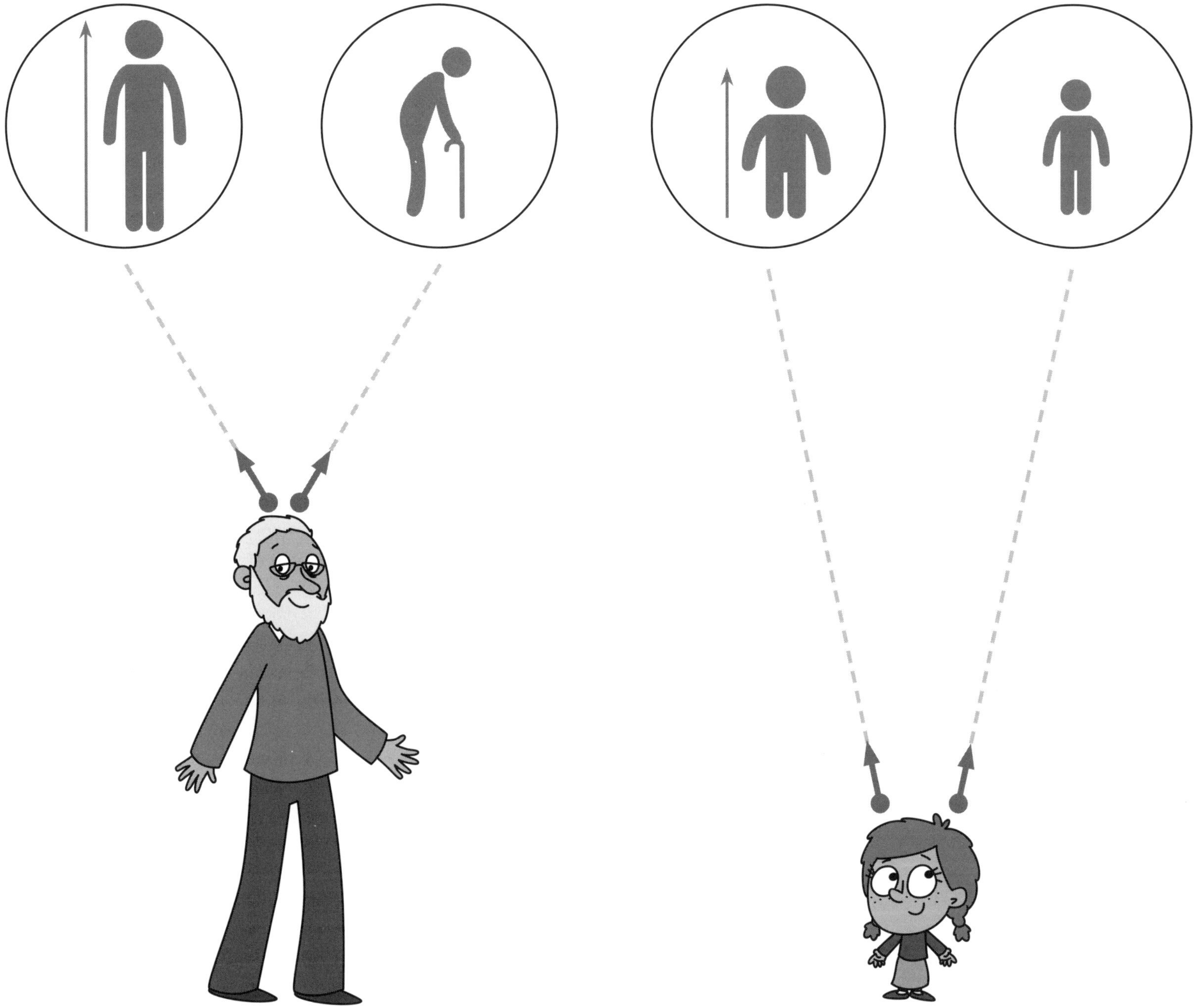

Language

Language: *What does he / she look like? He's / She's (short).* Point to the small pictures at the top and children say what each one represents: *(Tall. / Old. / Short. / Young.)* Point to the grandfather and ask: *Is he tall? Is he short? Is he old? Is he young?* Children draw lines to match the grandfather to the correct pictures. Repeat with the girl. Say: *(She's) (young).* Children point to the correct person. Invite children to say sentences for others to point.

✏️ Draw. 😃 Say.

Speaking

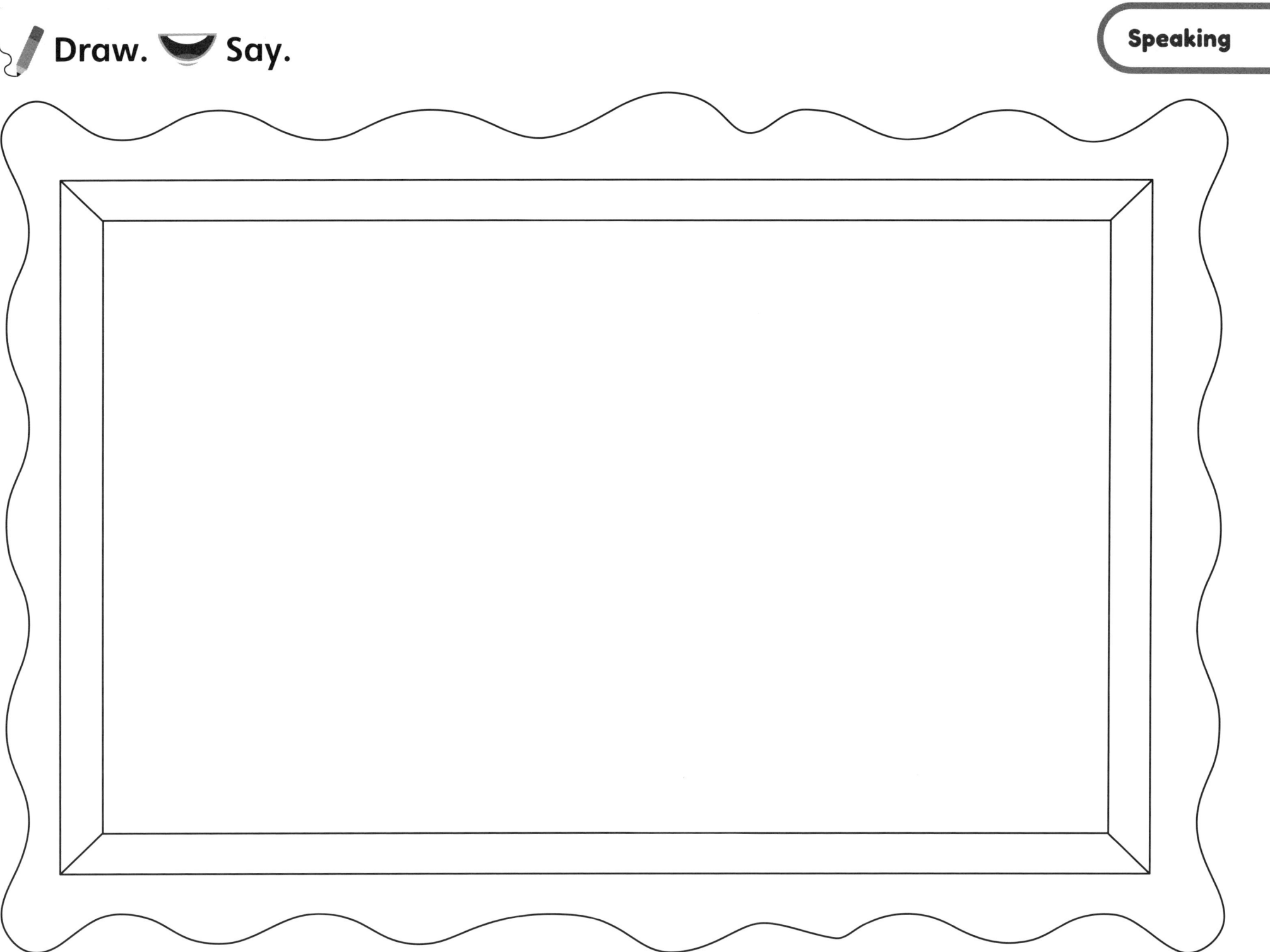

Language: *(She)'s my (mother). My (mother)'s name is (Maria).* Children choose someone from their family or a friend. They draw a picture of the person. They then point and say: *(She)'s my (mother). My (mother)'s name is (Maria).*

Unit 4

Match. Circle.

Cross-curricular: Science

Science: Learning to categorize animals by species. Look at the page together and ask: *Do animals have families? (Yes.)* Point to the first animal and say: *This is the mother. Help the mother find her baby.* Demonstrate by finger tracing how to trace the wavy line to the baby and say: *This is the baby!* Children trace the lines to match the adult and baby animals. Then, they circle all the baby animals on the page.

 Say. Trace. Count. Color.

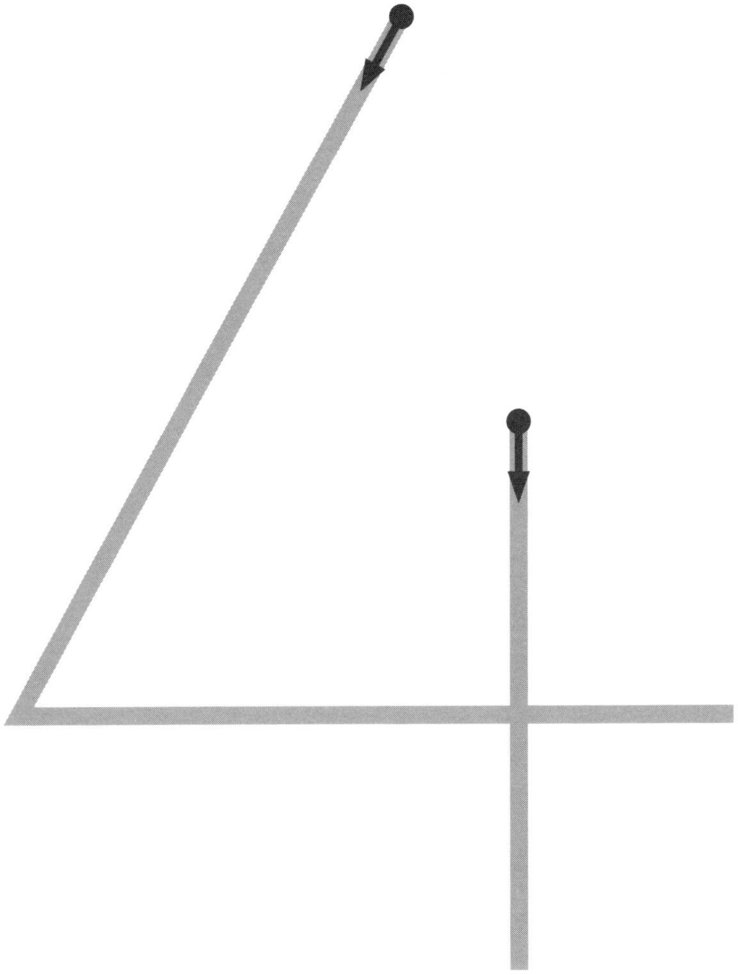

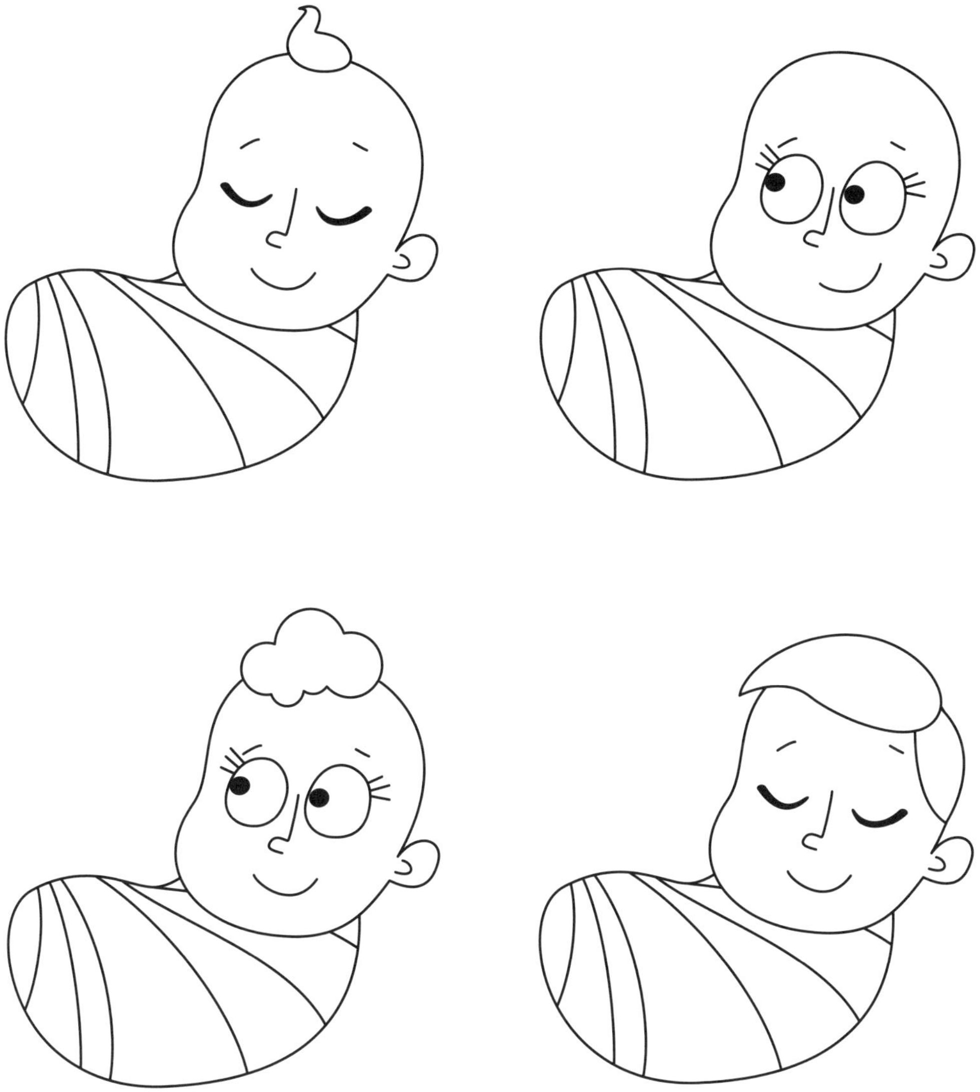

Numeracy

Numeracy: *four*. Children say the *Number 4 Chant* as they show four fingers: *Four, four, show me four. Show me four like this*. Then, children trace the number 4. Ask: *How many babies can you see? Let's count: one, two, three, four*. Repeat, encouraging children to count. Help children to count and choose four crayons and use them to color the babies.

Unit 4

 Say. Circle. Draw. Color.

Review

What is a family?

My favorite thing in Unit 4:

Unit 4

Vocabulary and Language Review: Ask the Big Question: *What is a family?* Children look back through Unit 4 to recall what they have learned. Ask them to look at the six pictures from Unit 4. They say the words and then circle the pictures that they are able to name. Accept all possible answers. Then ask: *What was your favorite thing in this unit?* Remind children of the song, story, cross-curricular lesson, etc. They draw a picture of their favorite thing. Children point to and talk about their pictures. Answer the Big Question together, using their pictures as a prompt. Finally, focus on the self-assessment activity. Ask: *How did you do in this unit?* Children color the face that shows how they feel they did.

5 What is a pet?

 Point. Stick. Color. Say.

Vocabulary: *cat, bird, rabbit, fish*. Say each new word, and children point to each animal as you say it. Say: *(Bird / Cat)*. *Stick the (bird / cat)*. Children stick each sticker as you say it. Then say: *(Fish / Rabbit)*. *Color the fish / rabbit*. Children color each animal as you say it. Finally, children point to and name each animal.

Unit 5

Say. Color.

Story

Unit 5

Language: *Is he / she (happy)? Yes, he / she is. No, he / she isn't. happy, sad.* Point to each picture. Ask questions about each character: *Is he / she (happy)?* Children answer: *Yes, he / she is.* or *No, he / she isn't.* They color the happy or sad face according to how the characters feel in each scene.

 Point. ◯ Circle. ◡ Say. ➤ Follow.

Phonics

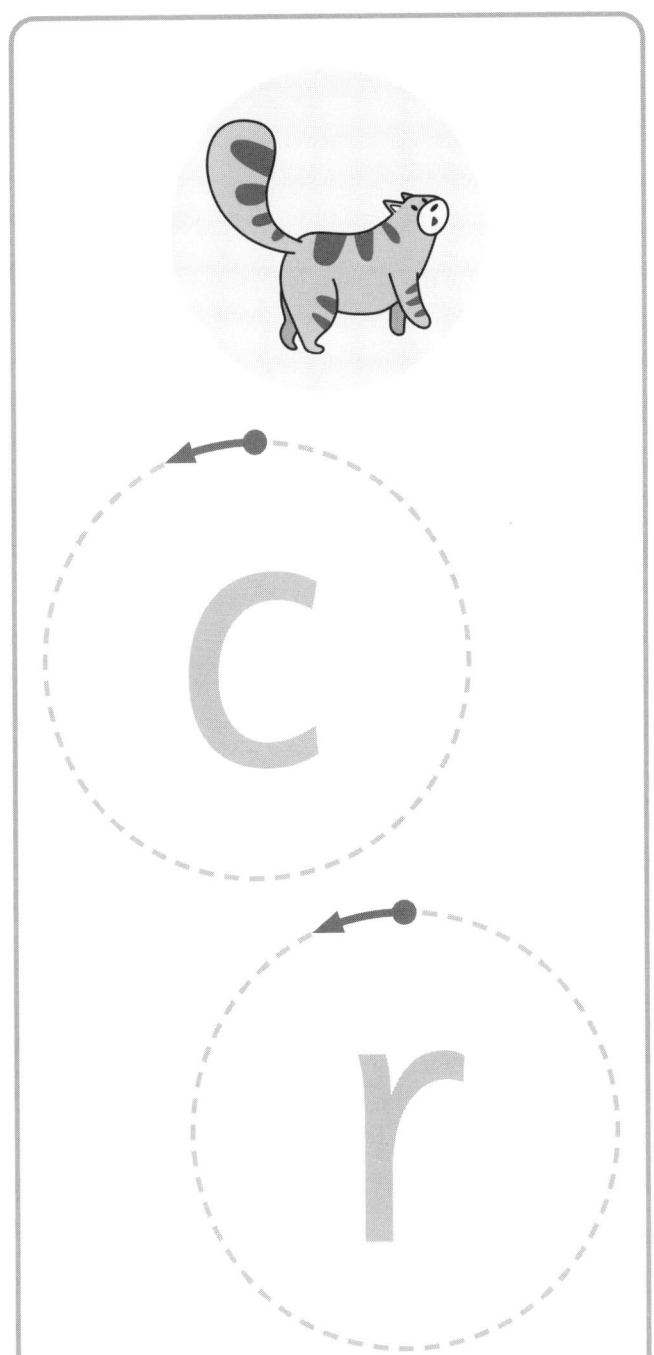
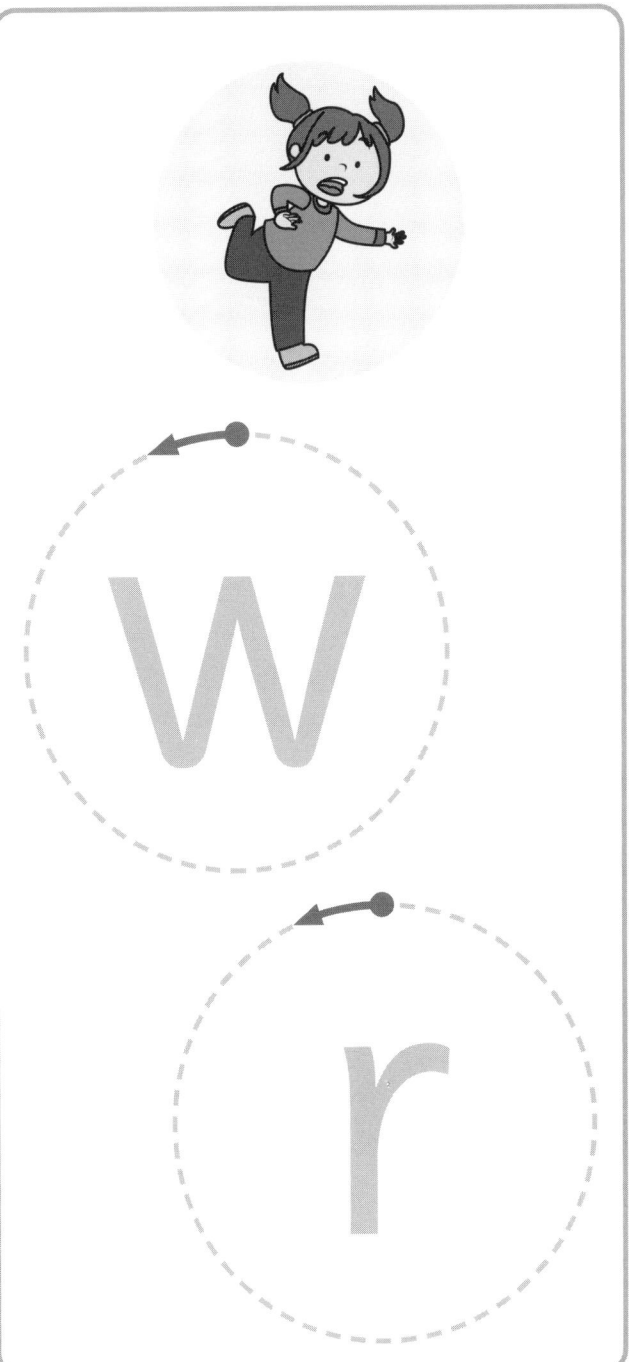
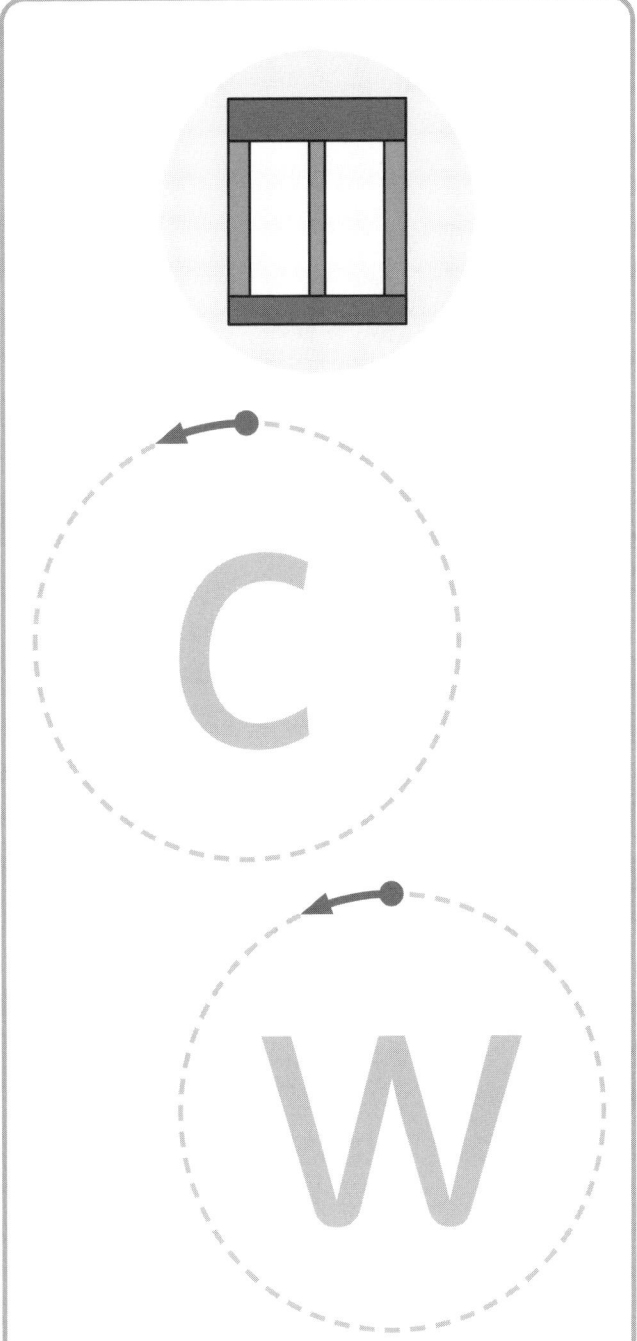

Phonics: *cat* /k/, *run* /r/, *window* /w/. Say the words in turn. Children point to the correct picture. Next, say the letter sounds /k/, /r/, /w/ for children to point to the correct letter and repeat the sounds. Children trace the circles to identify the correct letter for each picture, and say the words. Finally, children follow the letters with their finger, or, if they are ready, they can trace them with a pencil.

Unit 5

 Look. Circle. Color.

Literacy

Literacy: Identifying scenes from a story. Ask children to think about the story and remember what happens. Then focus on the pictures. Children look carefully, and identify and circle the five differences. Then ask: *Which picture is from the story?* Children color the circle of the correct picture.

Values: Taking care of our pets. Children look at the scene and and say what they see. Point to each child in the scene and ask: *Is he / she taking care of his / her pet?* Children identify and color the children who are taking care of the animals. They shouldn't color the girl who is walking away from the dog. They then point and name each pet.

 **Look.**  **Point.**   **Circle.** **Say.**

Vocabulary

Vocabulary: *turtle, dog, hamster, lizard.* Ask: *What can you see?* Point to each animal in section 1, and say: *Dog?* Highlight that the turtle is different, and children point to it. Children identify and point to the different animal in each section. They can circle them if they are able to. They then point to and name each animal.

 Count.  Match.  Say.

Language

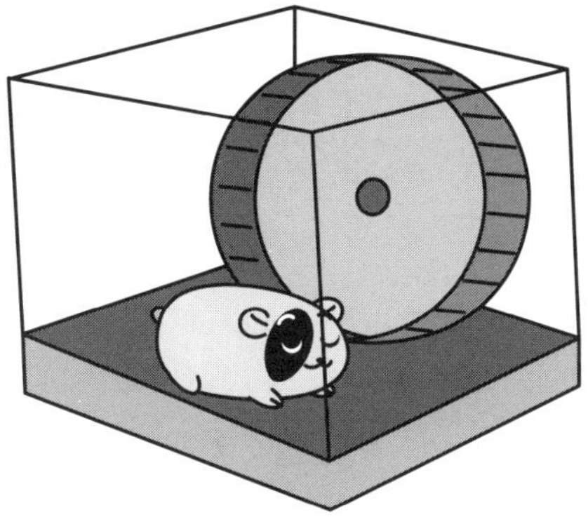

1 2 3 4

Language: *How many (birds) can you see? I can see (three birds).* Point to the first picture and ask: *How many birds can you see? Let's count.* Children draw a line to match the three birds to the number 3. Repeat with the other animals. Encourage children to say: *I can see (three birds).*

Unit 5

 **Draw.** **Say.**

Concept

Concept: *big / small*. Ask: *Is the cat big or small? (Big.)* Then say: *Let's draw a small cat!* and ask children to draw a small cat in the small empty box. Once they've finished, point to the small dog at the bottom of the page and ask: *Is the dog big or small? (Small.) Let's draw a big dog!* Ask children to draw a big dog in the big empty box. Finally, have children present their drawings and introduce them, e.g., *A small cat. A big dog.*

 Point.  Match.  Say.

Vocabulary

Vocabulary: *walk*, *jump*, *swim*, *fly*. Children point to the animals in the second column and name the actions: *swim*, *jump*, *walk*, *fly*. Then, they draw lines to match the silhouettes on the left to the animals on the right. Finally, they finger trace the lines and say the actions as they link the pictures, e.g., *swim – swim*, *jump – jump*.

Unit 5 67

 Language

Language: *Can (fish swim)? Yes, they can. No, they can't. (Fish) can (swim). (Fish) can't (walk).* Children look at each picture. Point to the fish and ask: *Can fish swim? Can fish walk?* Children answer *Yes, they can.* or *No, they can't.* Children circle the pictures showing things the animals can do. Finally, children say sentences about the animals, e.g., *Fish can swim. Fish can't walk.*

👆 **Point.** 👄 **Say.** 🖍 **Color.**

Speaking

Language: *What does a (dog) say? A (dog) says (woof, woof). woof, meow, blub, chirp.* Explain you are going to make sounds different animals make, and ask children to point to the correct animal. Say: *(Woof, woof!)* and children point to the (dog). Ask: *What does (a dog) say? (A dog says woof, woof.)* encouraging children to make the animal sounds. Children choose a different color for each animal, and color the animals. Then, they work in pairs. One child says: *(Red.)* and the other points to the correct animal and says: *A (fish) says (blub, blub).*

Unit 5

Look. Point. Circle. Say.

Cross-curricular: Science

Science: Learning to categorize animals as domestic or wild. Point to each animal and ask: *Is it a pet?* Encourage children to answer *Yes, it is.* or *No, it isn't.* Children point to each animal that is not a pet in each section. They can circle it if they are able to. Discuss wild animals and pets and how they are different.

 Say.  Trace.  Count. Color.

Numeracy

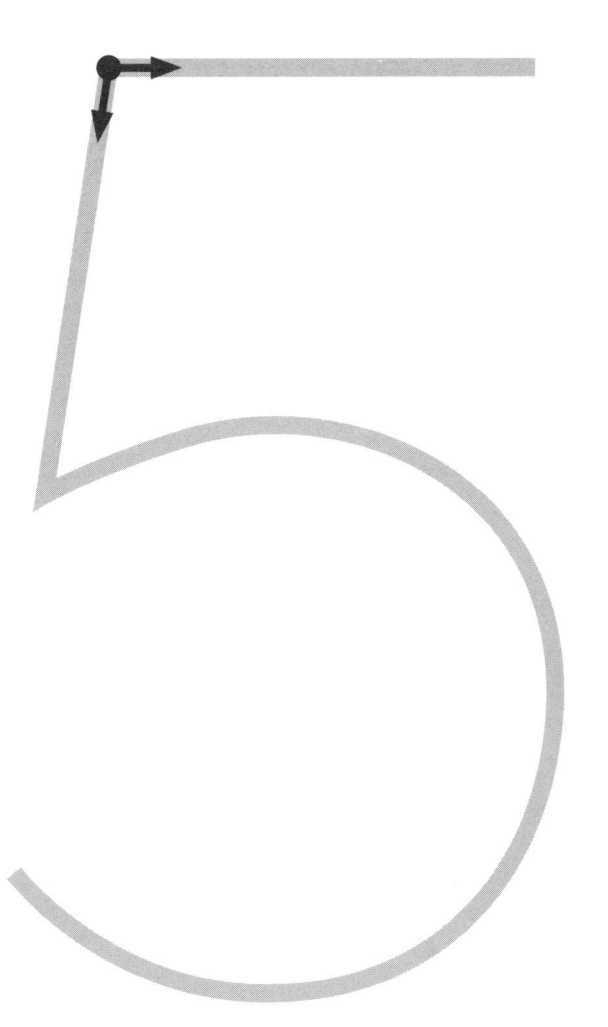

Numeracy: *five.* Children say the *Number 5 Chant* as they show five fingers: *Five, five, show me five. Show me five like this.* Then, they trace the number 5. Ask: *How many bubbles can you see? Let's count: one, two, three, four, five.* Repeat, encouraging children to count. Help children to count and choose five crayons and use them to color the bubbles.

Say. Circle. Draw. Color.

Review

What is a pet?

My favorite thing in Unit 5:

Unit 5

 What do we eat?

 Point. Stick. Color. Say.

Vocabulary: *apple, pear, tomato, carrot.* Say each new word, and children point to each food as you say it. Say: *(Pear / Tomato)*. *Stick the (pear / tomato).* Children stick each sticker as you say it. Then say: *(Carrot / Apple). Color the carrot / apple.* Children color each food as you say it. Finally, children point to and name each food.

Unit 6   73

◯ Circle. ᴗ Say.

Story

74 Unit 6 **Language:** *Does she (drink milk)? Yes, she does. No, she doesn't. apple, carrots, ice cream, milk.* Review the story with the children first. Children circle the pictures that show the food and drink Hannah has. Ask questions about each picture: *Does she (drink milk)?* Children answer: *Yes, she does.* or *No, she doesn't.*

 Point. Say. Circle. Follow.

Phonics

p

qu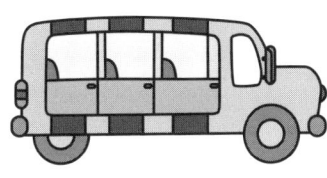

v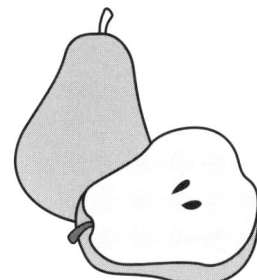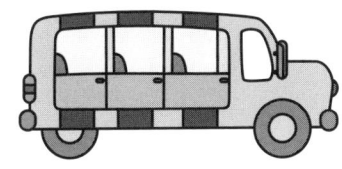

Phonics: *p*ear /p/, *qu*ail /kw/, *v*an /v/. Say the letter sounds /p/, /kw/, /v/. Children point to the correct letter(s) and repeat the sounds. Next, say the words for children to point to the correct picture. Children circle the correct picture for each letter sound, and say the words. Finally, children follow the letters with their finger, or, if they are ready, they can trace them with a pencil.

Unit 6 75

 Literacy

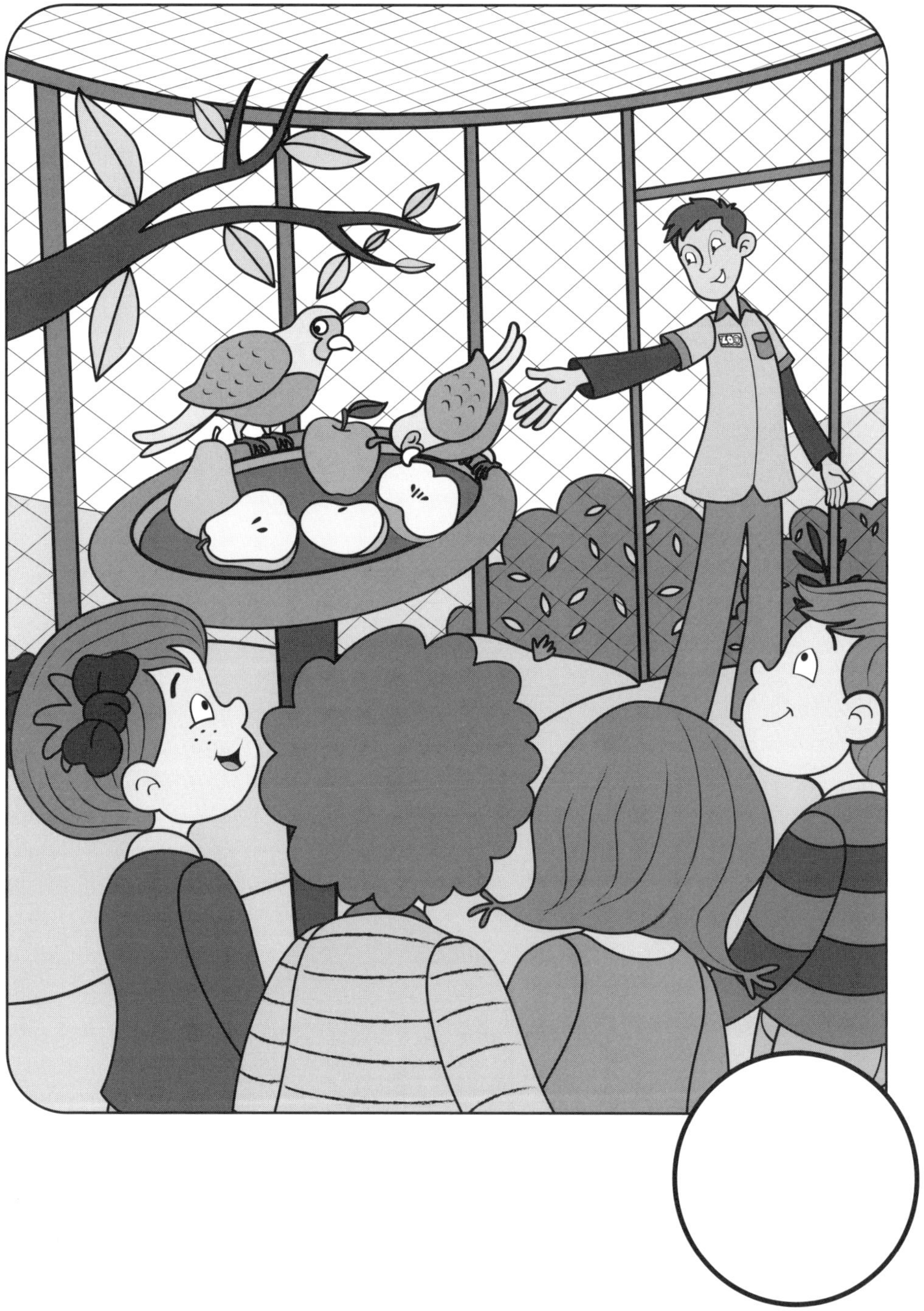

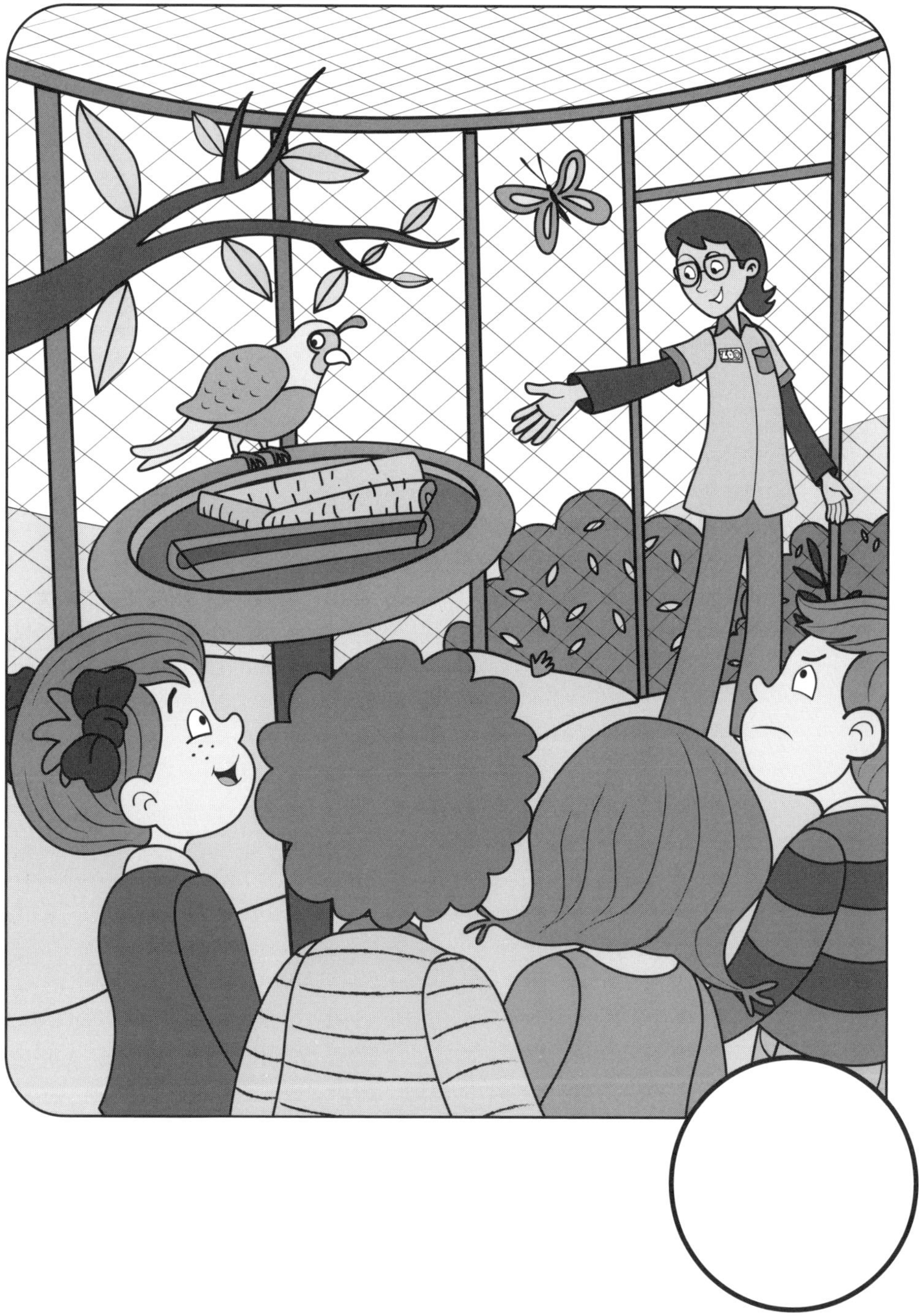

Literacy: Identifying scenes from a story. Ask children to think about the story and remember what happens. Then focus on the pictures. Children look carefully, and identify and point to the five differences. They can circle them if they are able to. Then ask: *Which picture is from the story?* Children color the circle of the correct picture.

👆 **Point.** ⭕ **Circle.** 😊 **Say.**

Values

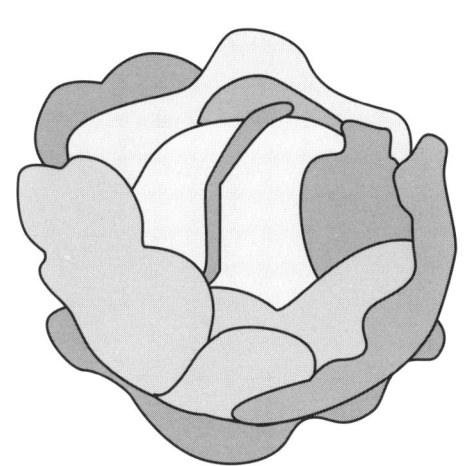

Values: Washing fruit and vegetables. Children point to and name the fruit and vegetables. Point to the apple and ask: *Do we wash apples? (Yes.)* Point to the banana and ask: *Do we wash bananas? (No.)* Discuss with children why we don't wash some fruits and vegetables. Children look and circle the fruit and vegetables that we do wash. Then, they point and say: *We wash (apples).*

Unit 6 77

 **Point. Say. Draw.**

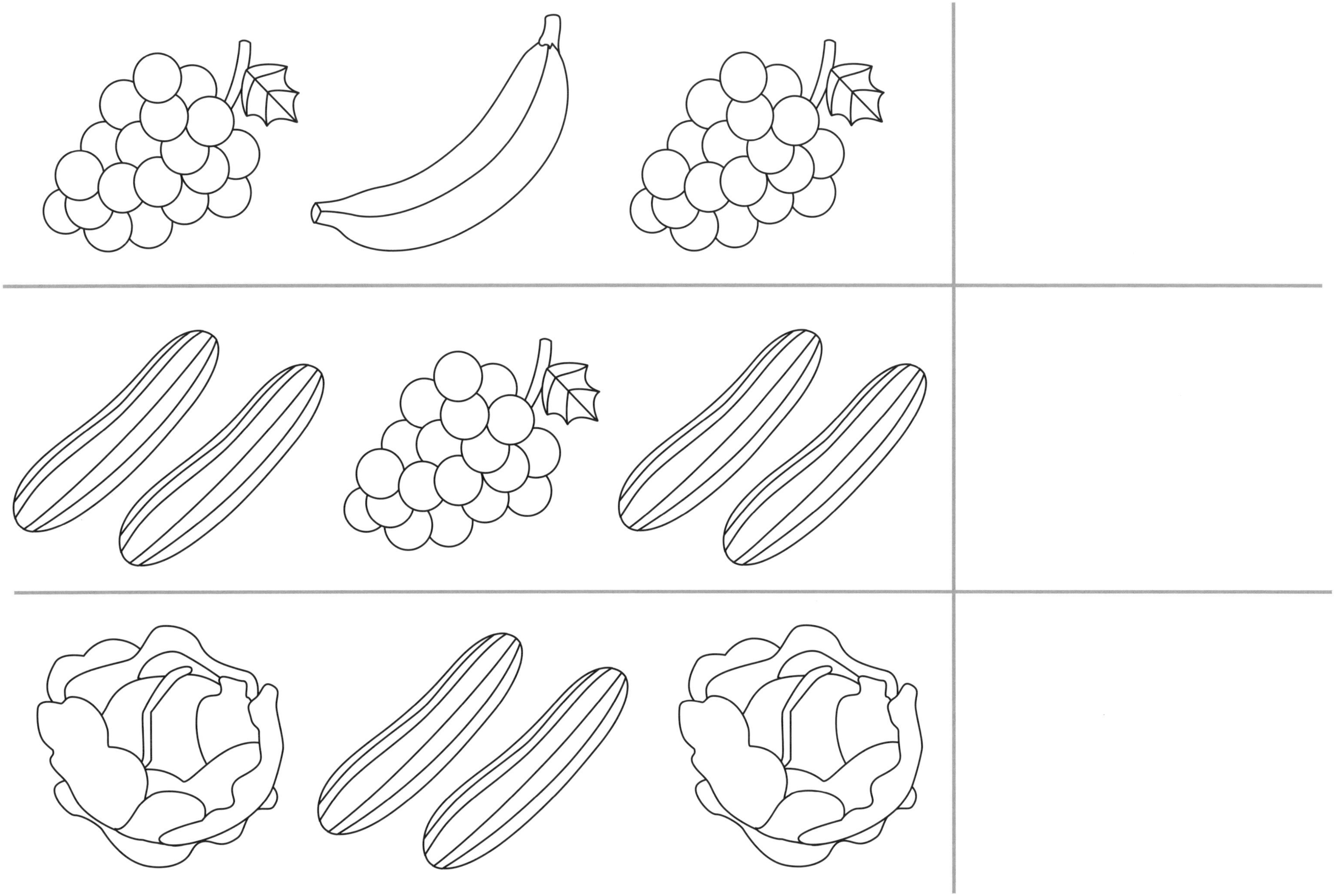

Vocabulary

Vocabulary: bananas, grapes, cucumbers, lettuce. Children point to and name the foods: *grapes, banana, cucumbers, lettuce*. Then, they look at the pattern in each row and say what food should come next. Guide them through the first pattern. Say: *grapes, banana, grapes … What comes next? (Banana.)* Children draw a banana in the empty space. Continue with the other rows. Once children have finished drawing, ask them to repeat the completed patterns, e.g., *grapes – banana – grapes – banana*.

Unit 6

Draw. Color. Say.

Language

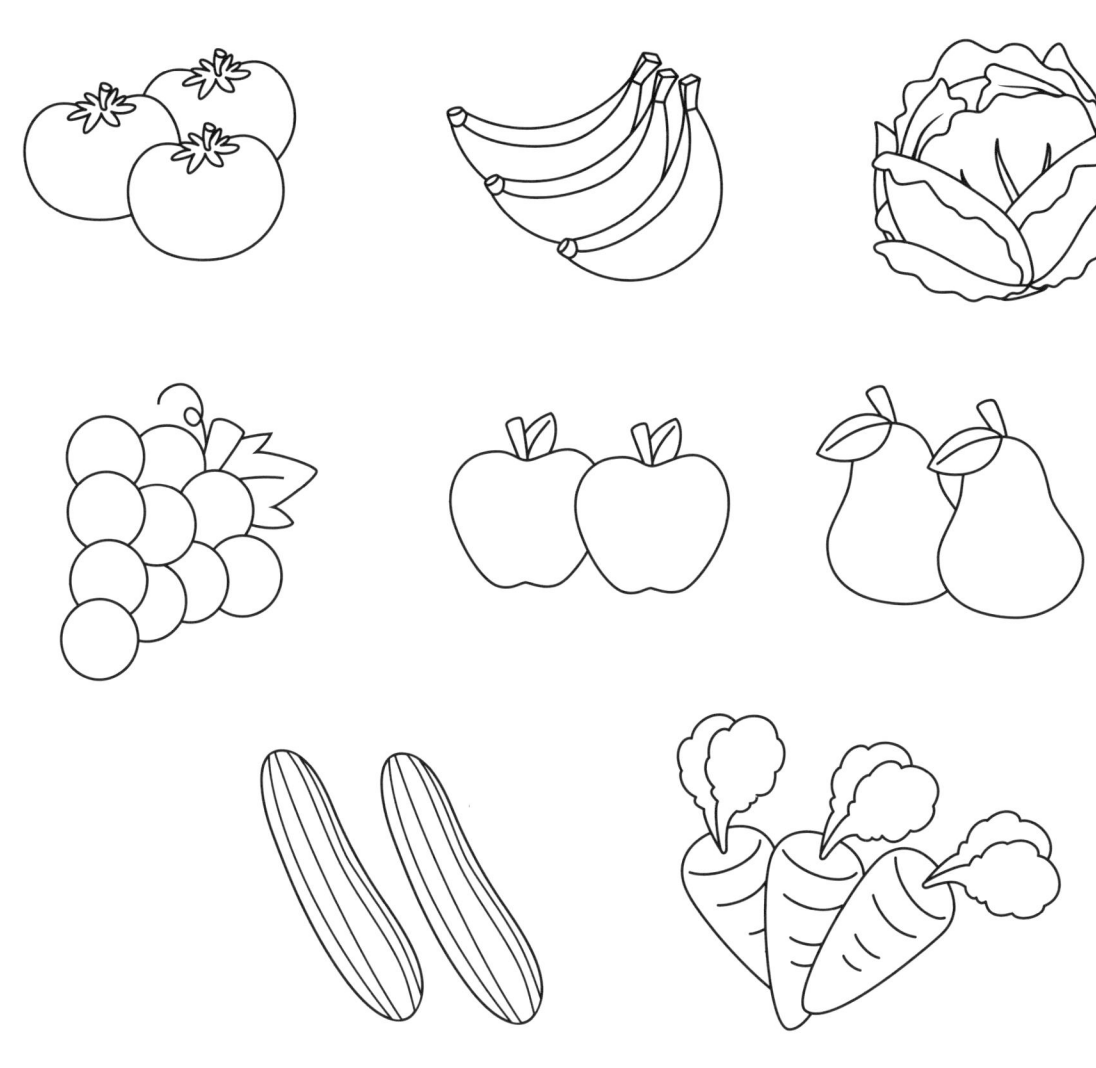

Language: *Which foods do you like? I like (bananas).* Children look at all the food items. Ask: *Which foods do you like?* Accept answers from some volunteers. Explain they can draw and color the child on the page to look like themselves and then color the food they like. Finally, children present their finished page and say which foods they like, e.g., *I like apples.*

 Say. Trace. Color.

Concept

Concept: Identifying circles. Point to each food item and ask: *What shape is it?* Finger trace a circle and say: *Circle.* Children copy you, finger tracing in the air and saying: *circle, circle, circle.* Then, point to each item on the page and ask: *Is it a circle? (Yes. / No.)* Children trace the circles and color the circular food items.

 **Look.**  **Circle.**  **Say.**

Vocabulary

  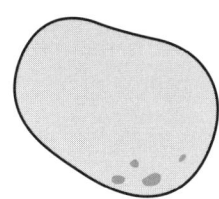

 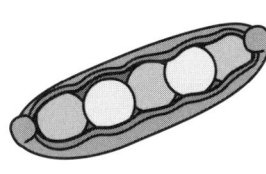  

  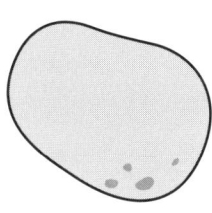 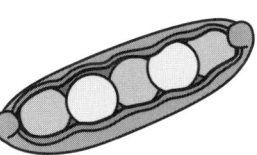

 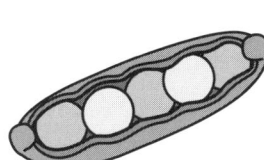  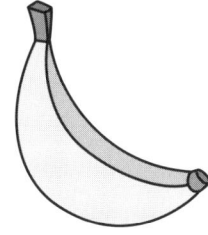

Vocabulary: *pineapple, orange, potato, peas.* Children point to and name the food items. Point to the silhouette on the top row, and ask children what food it represents *(Pineapple.).* They find and circle the picture that matches the silhouette. Repeat with the other three rows. Point to each food and ask children: *Do you like (pineapples)?*

Unit 6 81

 Draw. Color. Say.

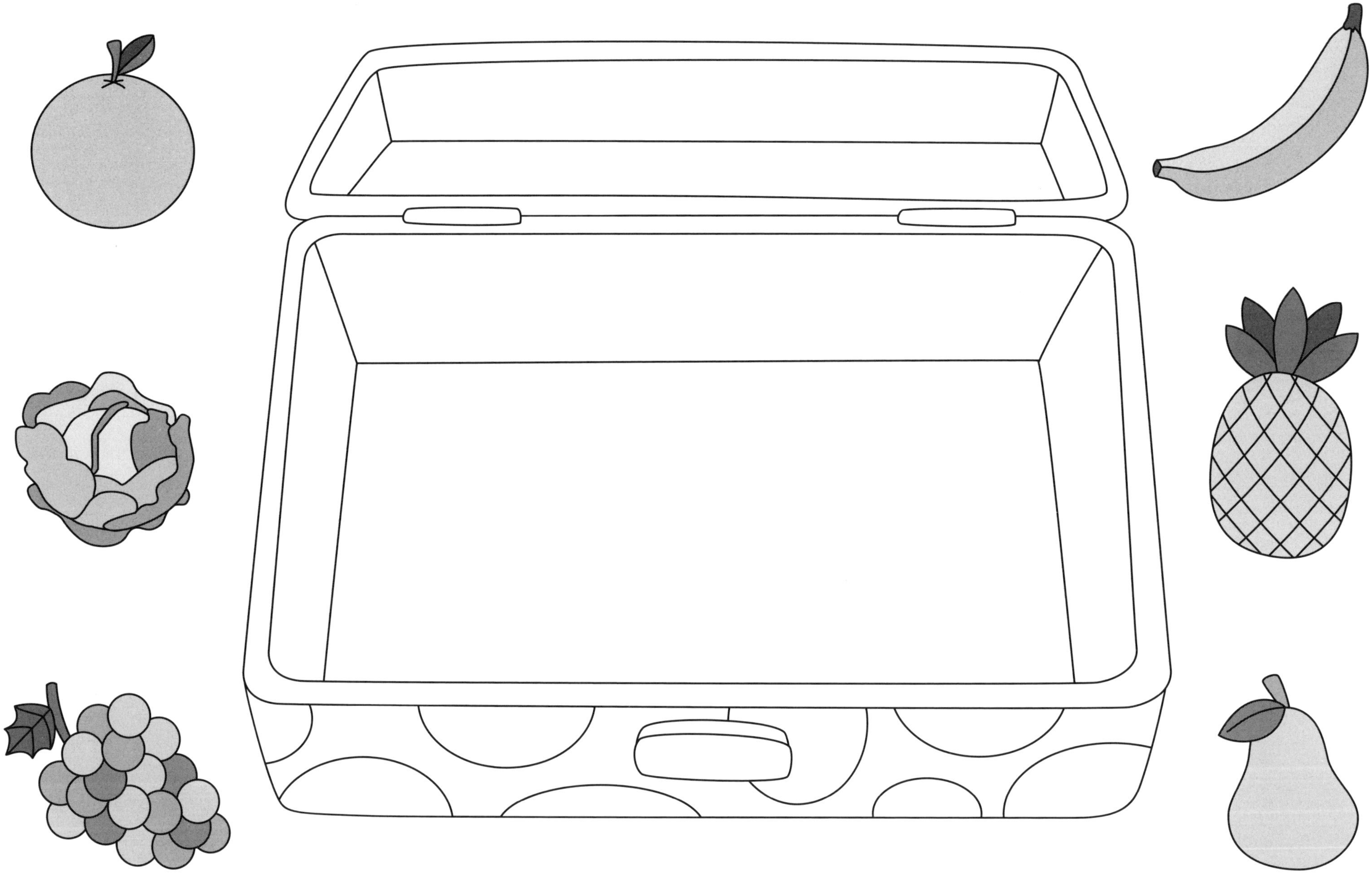

Language

Language: *What do you have? I have (an orange).* Point to the food items around the lunchbox and children name them. Children draw and color two food items in the lunchbox. Then, they present their finished drawings and answer the question: *What do you have in your lunchbox?* using the structure *I have (an orange)*.

✏️ Color. 👄 Say.

Speaking

Language: *Do you like (pineapples)? Yes, I do. No, I don't. I like (oranges).* Point to the foods and ask: *Do you like (pineapples)?* Encourage children to answer with *Yes, I do.* or *No, I don't.* Children look at each food and color the happy face if they like it, and the sad face if they don't like it. Finally, they say what they like, e.g., *I like oranges.*

Unit 6 | 83

Match. **Color.** **Say.**

Cross-curricular: Science

Science: Learning what trees need to grow. Point to the apple tree and ask children: *What does it need?* Point to each smaller picture and ask them, one at a time: *Does it need (sun)?* Children draw lines from the tree to the things it needs to grow. Finally, they color the tree to illustrate it flourishing now that it has what it needs, and practice saying, e.g., *It needs soil*.

 Say. Trace. Count. Color.

Numeracy

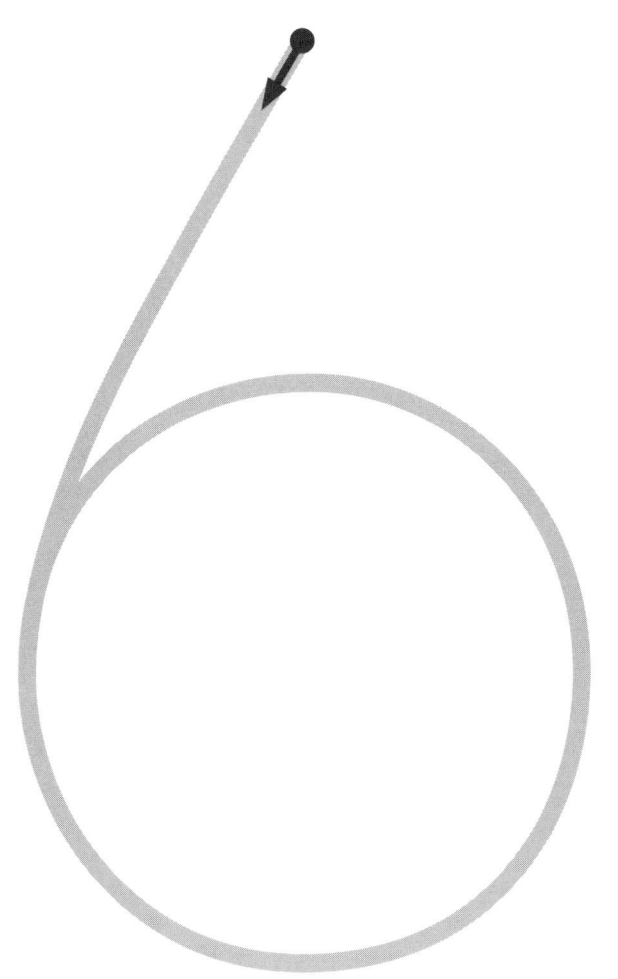

Numeracy: *six*. Children say the *Number 6 Chant* as they show six fingers: *Six, six, show me six. Show me six like this*. Then, they trace the number 6. Ask: *How many bananas can you see? Let's count. One, two, three, four, five, six*. Repeat, encouraging children to count. Help children to count and choose six crayons and use them to color the bananas.

Unit 6 • 85

Say. Circle. Draw. Color.   Review

What do we eat?

My favorite thing in Unit 6:

Unit 6

Vocabulary and Language Review: Ask the Big Question: *What do we eat?* Children look back through Unit 6 to recall what they have learned. Ask them to look at the six pictures from Unit 6. They say the words and then circle the pictures that they are able to name. Then ask: *What was your favorite thing in this unit?* Remind children of the song, story, cross-curricular lesson, etc. They draw a picture of their favorite thing. Children point to and talk about their pictures. Answer the Big Question together, using their pictures as a prompt. Finally, focus on the self-assessment activity. Ask: *How did you do in this unit?* Children color the face that shows how they feel they did.

7 What is a toy?

 Point. Stick. Color.  Say.

Vocabulary: *car, teddy bear, doll, ball.* Say each new word, and children point to each toy as you say it. Say: *(Ball / Car)*. *Stick the (ball / car)*. Children stick each sticker as you say it. Then say: *(Doll / Teddy bear)*. *Color the doll / teddy bear*. Children color each toy as you say it. Finally, children point to and name each toy.

Unit 7

 Say. Circle.

Story

Language: *Is it in the story? Yes, it is. No, it isn't.* Ask children to remember the story. Point to each picture and ask: *Is it in the story?* Children answer: *Yes, it is.* or *No, it isn't.* They circle the things that are in the story (*ant, dragonfly, yo-yo*).

👆 **Point.** 👄 **Say.** ✨ **Match.** ➡ **Follow.**

Phonics

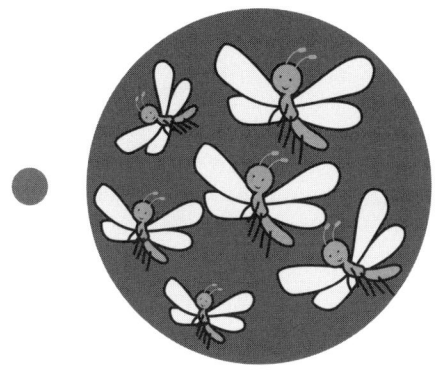

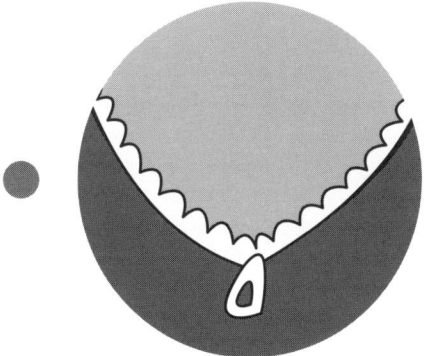

Phonics: *six* /ks/, *yo-yo* /j/, *zipper* /z/. Say the letter sounds /ks/, /j/, /z/. Children point to the correct letter and repeat the sounds. Repeat with the words and pictures (*six, yo-yo, zipper*). Next, say the letter sounds for children to point to the correct picture, or say the words and children point to the correct letter. Children match the letters to the pictures, and say the words. Finally, children follow the letters with their finger, or, if they are ready, they can trace them with a pencil.

 Look.  Match. Say.

Literacy

Literacy: Identifying the sequence of a story. Ask children to think about the story and remember what happens. Then focus on the story at the bottom of the page, and the missing pictures above it. Children look carefully and match the frames to the sequence. They then say as much of the story as they can remember, using the pictures as prompts.

👁 Look. ✏️ Color. 😊 Say.

Values

Values: Sharing our toys. Children look at the scene. Ask: *What are the children doing? (Playing.)* Point to each child in the scene and ask: *Is he / she sharing the toys?* Children identify and color the children who are sharing the toys. They then point to the children sharing their toys and say: *He's / She's sharing the (blocks).*

 Point.  Match.  Say.

Vocabulary

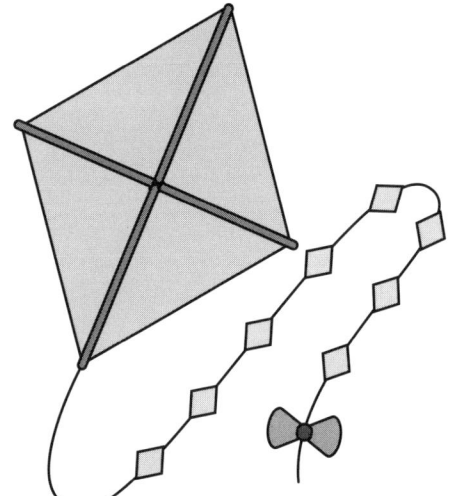

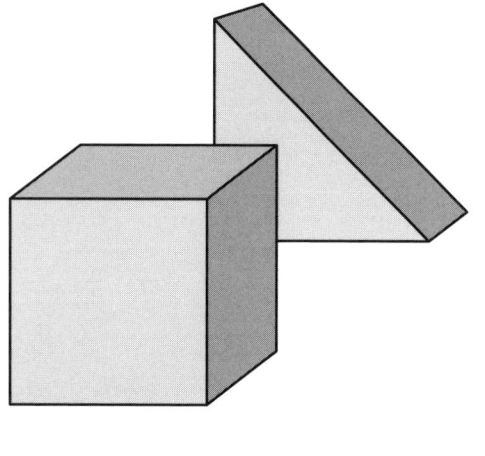
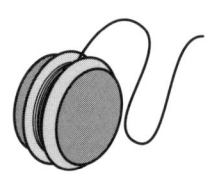

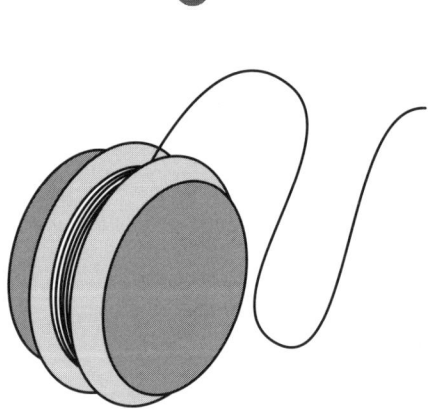
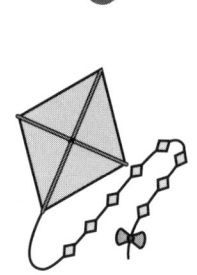

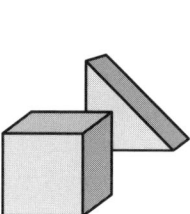

Vocabulary: *kite, tricycle, blocks, yo-yo.* Children point to and name the toys in the top row: *kite, tricycle, blocks, yo-yo.* Then, they draw lines to match the corresponding big and small toys. Finally, children finger trace the lines and say the words as they link the pictures, e.g., *big kite – small kite.*

Color. Trace. Say. Language

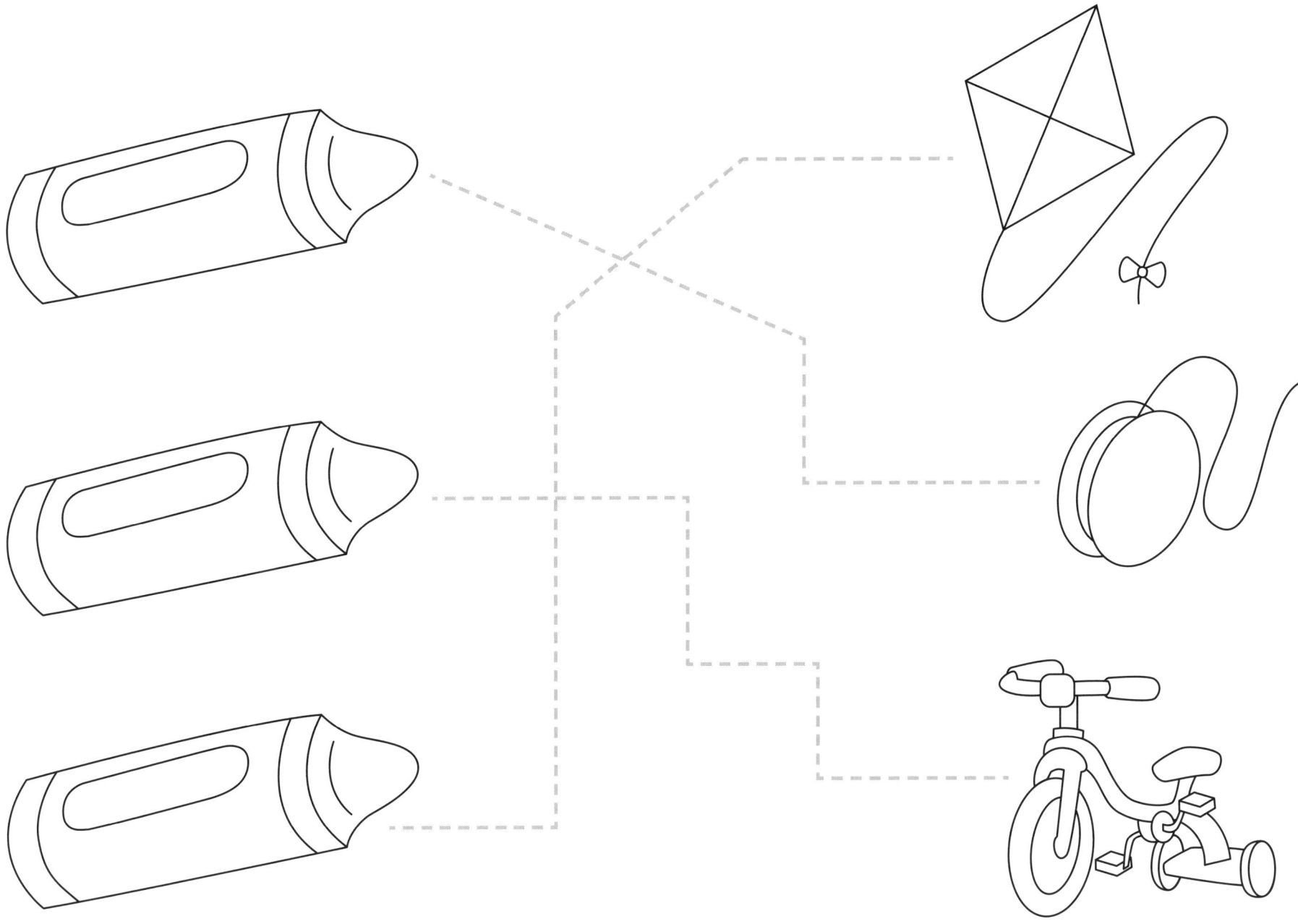

Language: *What color is the (yo-yo)? It's (red).* Have children choose three colors and color the crayons. Then, they trace the lines and color the toys in the corresponding colors. Finally, ask: *What color is the (kite)?* Encourage children to respond by saying: *It's (yellow). / The (kite) is (yellow).*

Unit 7

 Look. Say. Color. Trace.

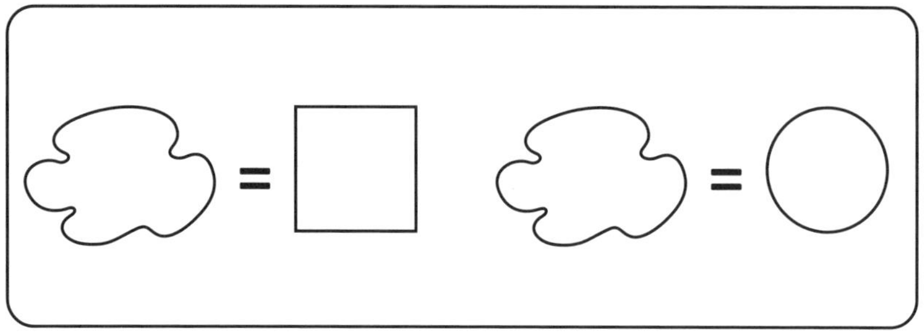

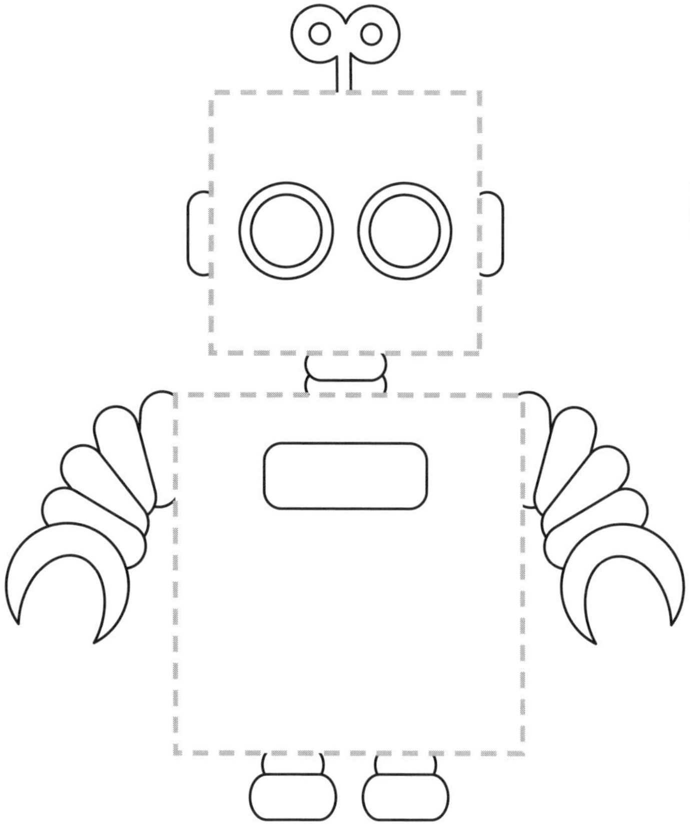

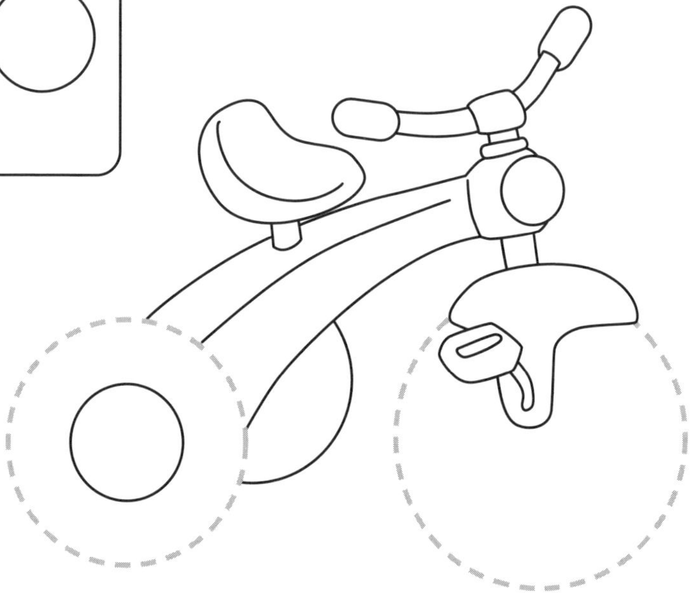

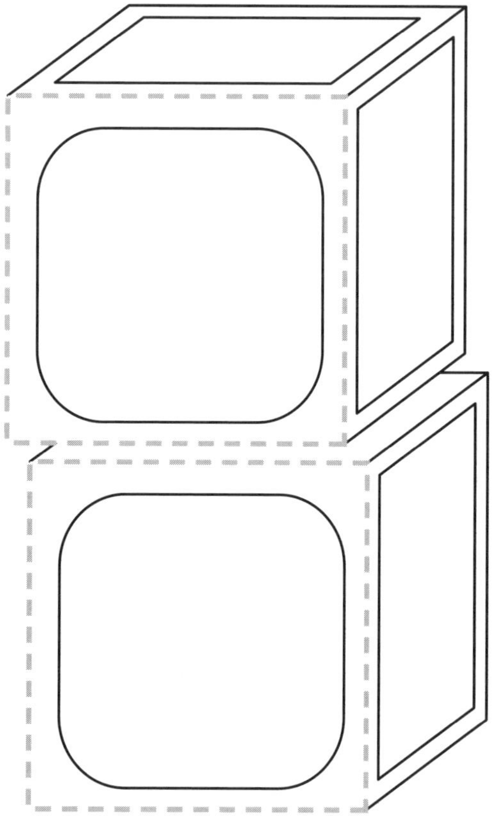

Concept

Concept: Identifying squares and circles. Children look at the first picture. Ask: *What is it? (A tricycle.) What shape are the (wheels)? (Circles.)* Repeat with the other pictures. Children choose two colors to represent *square* and *circle*, and complete the key at the top of the page. They then trace each shape in the correct color, according to their key.

94 Unit 7

 **Vocabulary**

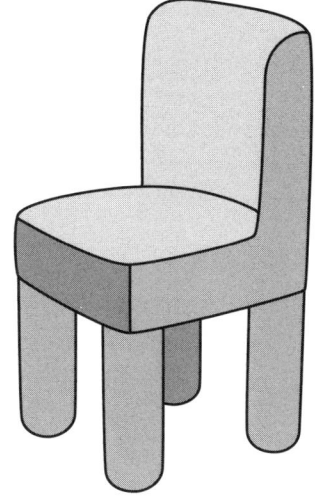  

 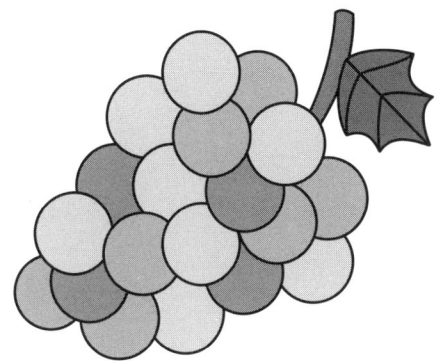 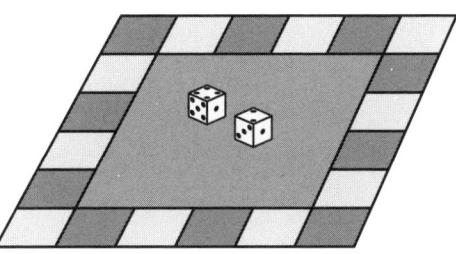

Vocabulary: *train, puzzle, board game, robot.* Children point to and name the items. Ask: *What is a toy?* Children respond by pointing to or by naming one of the toys on the page. Point to each item and ask: *Is it a toy?* Children circle the toys. They say: *It's a (train).*

Unit 7 95

 Look. Color. Say.

Language

1 red 2 yellow 3 blue

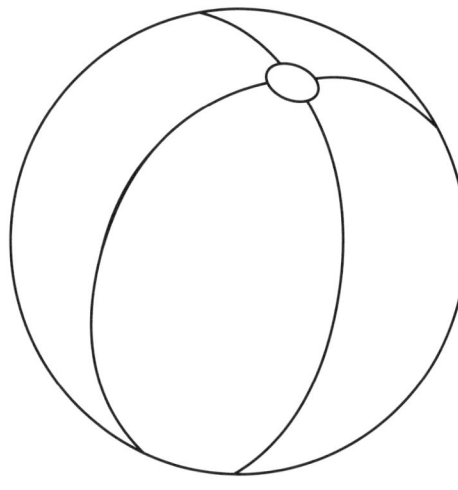

Language: *The (ball) is (big) and (blue).* Explain to children they are going to color the toys three different colors. Distribute crayons, and tell them to color the circle beside number 1 red, circle 2 yellow, and circle 3 blue. Then have them color the toys using the color key as a guide. Finally, children say sentences about the toys, e.g., *The ball is big and blue.*

 Match. ⭕ Circle. 😊 Say.

Speaking

Language: *I want a (teddy bear), please. Here you are. Thank you.* Point to the wrapped presents, and say: *Is it a (ball)?* Children draw lines to match each wrapped present to the correct toy. Ask: *Which toy do you want?* Children circle the toy they want. Then they answer: *I want a (tricycle), please.*

Unit 7 97

 **Look. Match. Say.**

Cross-curricular: Science

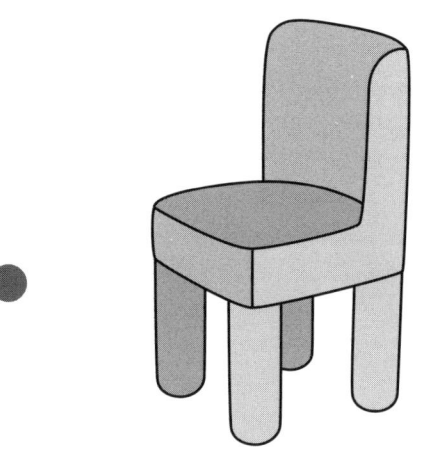

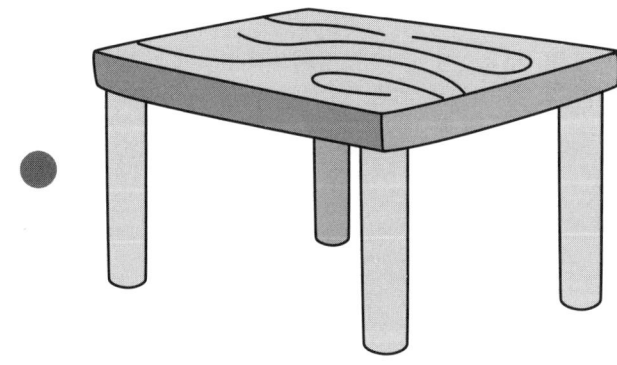

Science: Learning that toys are made of different materials. Point to each toy on the left. Ask: *What's it made of?* Refer to page 98 in the Student's Book if necessary. Children answer: *It's made of (plastic)*. Then point to each item on the right and ask the same question. Children match the toy on the left to the item on the right that is made of the same material. Encourage them to say: *They're made of (plastic)*.

 Say. Trace. Count. Color.

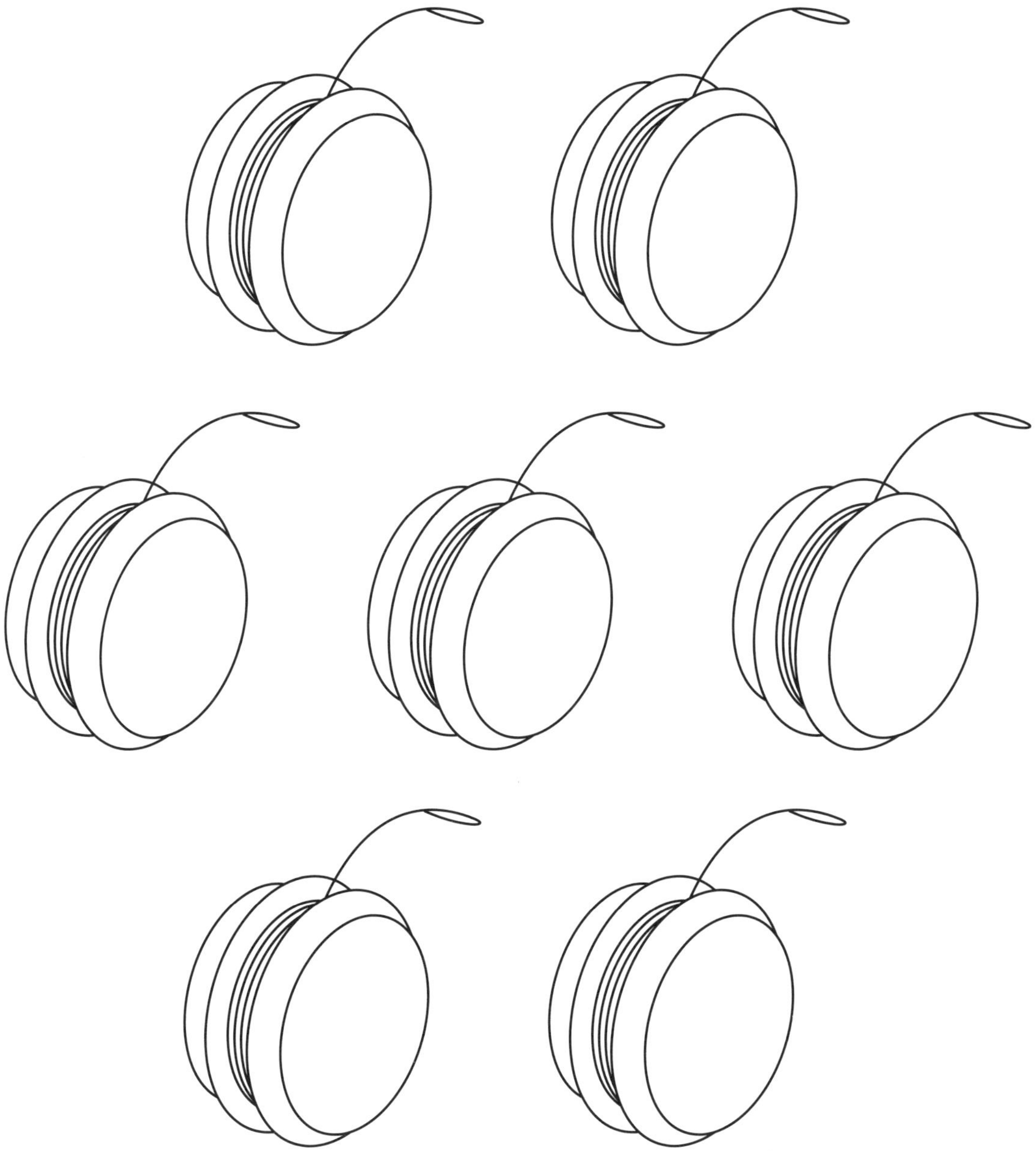

Numeracy

Numeracy: *seven*. Children say the *Number 7* Chant as they show seven fingers: *Seven, seven, show me seven. Show me seven like this.* Then, they trace the number 7. Ask: *How many yo-yos can you see? Let's count: One, two, three, four, five, six, seven.* Repeat, encouraging children to count. Help children to count and choose seven crayons and use them to color the yo-yos.

Unit 7

Say. Circle. Draw. Color.   Review

What is a toy?

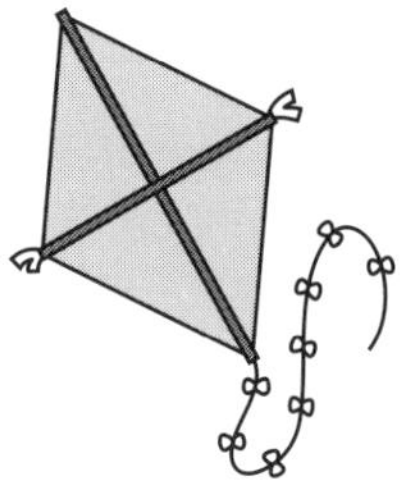

My favorite thing in Unit 7:

Unit 7

Vocabulary and Language Review: Ask the Big Question: *What is a toy?* Children look back through Unit 7 to recall what they have learned. Ask them to look at the six pictures from Unit 7. They say the words and then circle the pictures that they are able to name. Then ask: *What was your favorite thing in this unit?* Remind children of the song, story, cross-curricular lesson, etc. They draw a picture of their favorite thing. Children point to and talk about their pictures. Answer the Big Question together, using their pictures as a prompt. Finally, focus on the self-assessment activity. Ask: *How did you do in this unit?* Children color the face that shows how they feel they did.

 # What can we see in a park?

 Point.   Stick.   Color.   Say.

Vocabulary: *tree, flower, grass, bee.* Say each new word, and children point to each item as you say it. Say: *(Bee / Flower).* Stick the *(bee / flower).* Children stick each sticker as you say it. Then say: *(Tree / Grass). Color the tree / grass.* Children color each item as you say it. Finally, children point to and name each item.

 Match. Say.

Story

Language: *Where's the (teddy bear)? It's (on) the (swing). ant, iguana, teddy bear, sandbox, swing, tree.* Ask children to think about the story and remember what happens. Children draw lines to match the animal / toy to the place where it is in the story. Point to the picture of the teddy bear. Ask: *Where's the teddy bear?* Children answer: *It's on the swing.* Repeat for the other two pictures.

 **Point.** **Say.** **Circle.** **Follow.** | Phonics

Phonics: *a*nt /æ/, *i*guana /ɪ/, *u*mbrella /ʌ/. Say the words in turn. Children point to the correct picture. Next, say the letter sounds /æ/, /ɪ/, /ʌ/ for children to point to the correct letter and repeat the sounds. Children circle the correct letter for each picture, and say the words. Finally, children follow the letters with their finger, or, if they are ready, they can trace them with a pencil.

Unit 8

 **Look. Match. Say.**

Literacy

Literacy: Identifying the sequence of a story. Ask children to think about the story and remember what happens. Then focus on the story at the bottom of the page, and the missing pictures above it. Children look carefully and match the frames to the sequence. They then say what happens first / next / last, using the pictures as prompts.

Look. Match. Say.

Values

Values: Keeping parks clean. Children look at the scene. Ask: *What are they doing? (Keeping the park clean.)* Children find the garbage in the park and draw lines to match it to the garbage bag. Discuss why it is important to keep our parks clean (e.g., so everyone can enjoy them). Discuss what we can do to keep our parks clean (e.g., pick up and throw garbage in the garbage can).

Unit 8

Point. Trace.  Say.

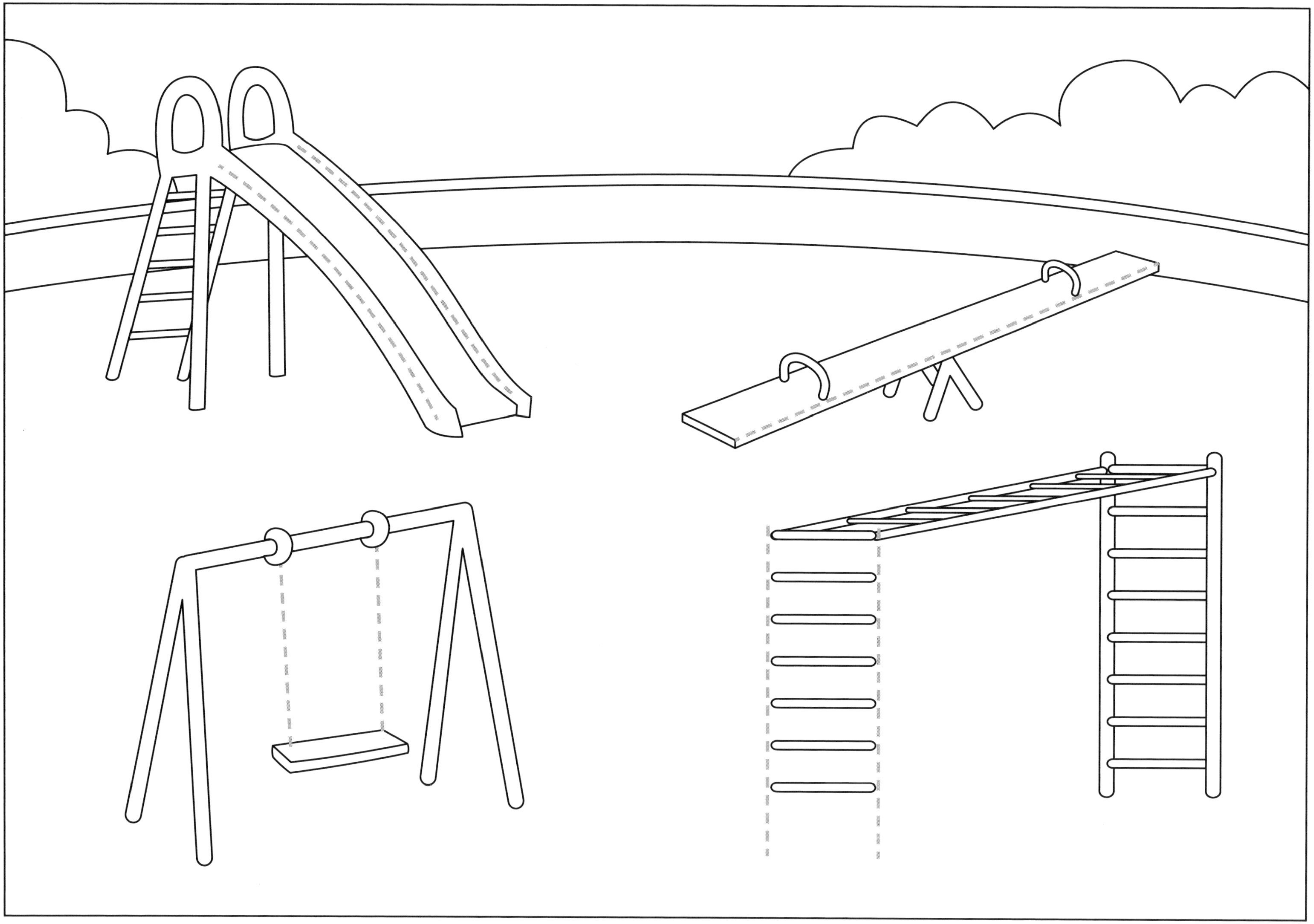

Vocabulary

Vocabulary: *swing, slide, seesaw, monkey bars.* Children point to and name the playground items. Then, they trace the lines to complete the pictures, while repeating their names.

 Say. Color.

Language

Language: *Do you like to play on the (swing)? Yes, I do. No, I don't.* Point to each playground item and ask: *Do you like to play on the (seesaw)?* Encourage children to answer with *Yes, I do.* or *No, I don't.* Children look at each playground item and color the happy face if they like it, and the sad face if they don't like it.

👁 Look. 🖍 Color. ✏ Trace.

Concept

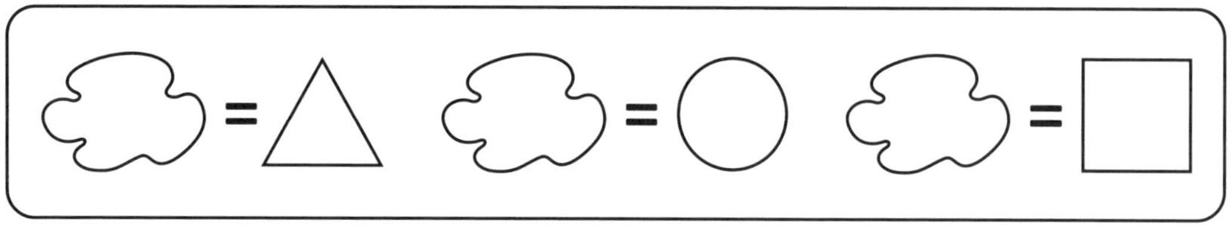

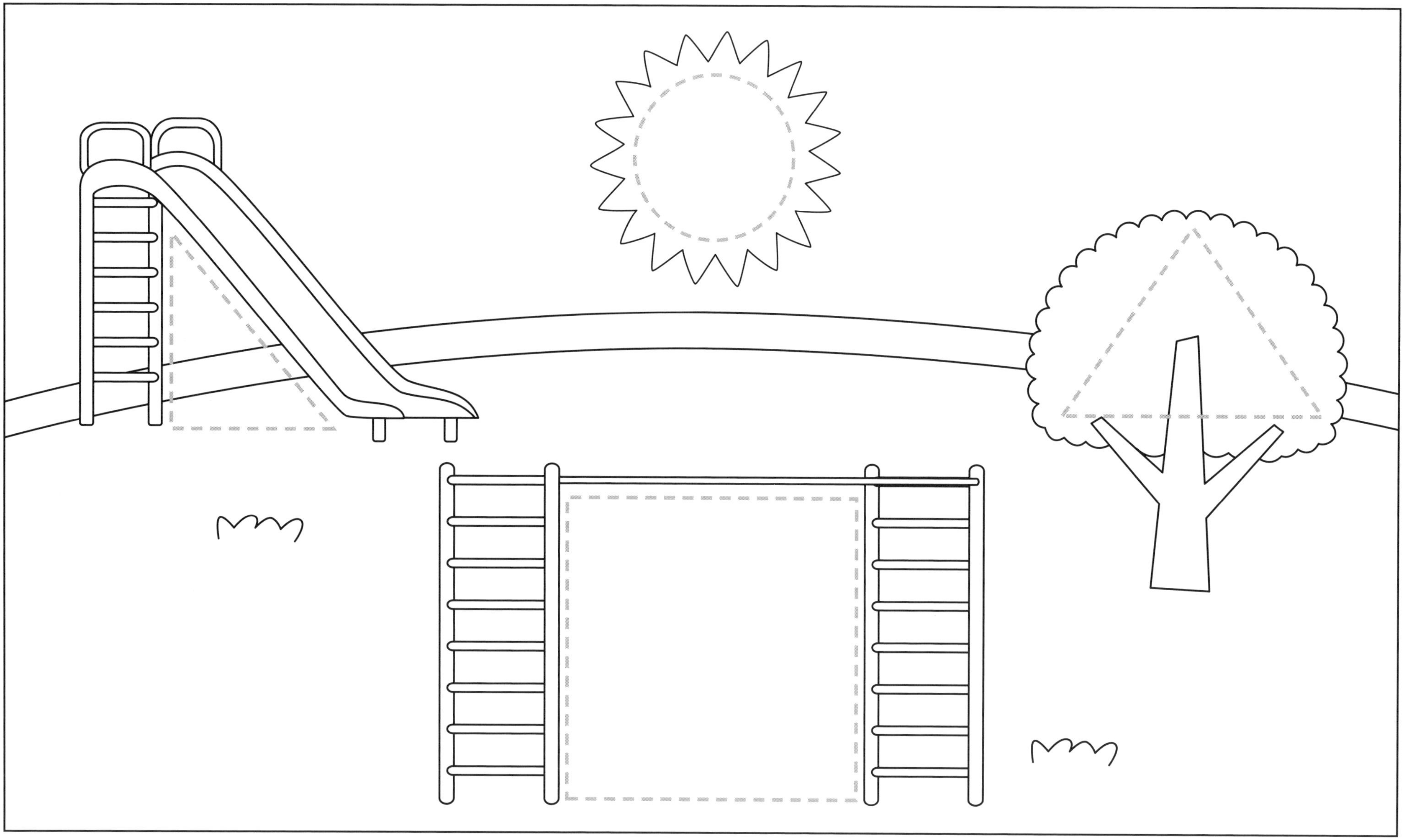

Color. Say.

Vocabulary

Vocabulary: *sun, cloud, sky, butterfly*. Point to the new vocabulary items and ask: *What's this?* Children name the items. Then, children color the sky, sun, cloud, and butterfly. As they're working, go around, point to the items, and encourage children to repeat after you.

Unit 8

👁 Look. ⟳ Circle. ᴗ Say.

Language

Language: *There's a (butterfly). There are some (clouds).* Focus on the pictures. Children look carefully, and identify and circle the five differences. Then ask: *What can you see?* Children point to a difference and say: *There's a (sun). There are some (clouds).*

Color. Say.

Speaking

Language: *There's a (sun). What does it look like? It's (big and yellow).* Children point to and name the objects. Distribute red, blue, yellow, and green crayons, holding each up and asking: *What color is it?* Children color the items as they like. Finally, children present their pages. Ask: *What is there?* Children answer: *There's a (sun).* Ask: *What does it look like?* Children answer: *It's (big and yellow).* Finally, children practice asking the questions.

Unit 8 — 111

 **Look. Draw. Say.**

Cross-curricular: Math

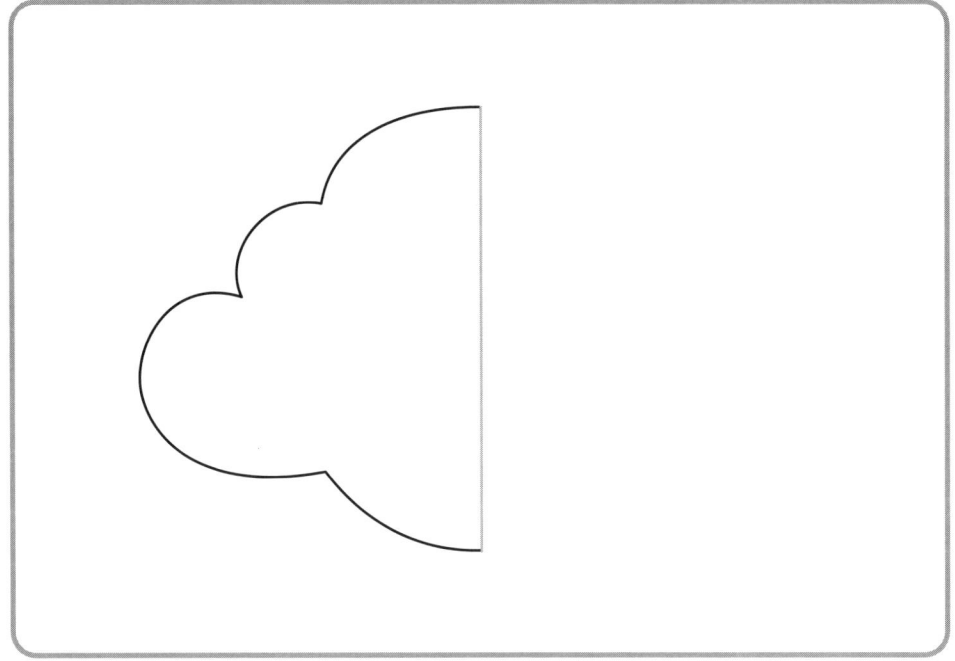

Math: Learning to recognize symmetry. Ask children what they think the pictures show. Children complete the second half of each picture so that both sides are the same. They then point and name the objects.

 Say. Trace. Count. Color.

Numeracy

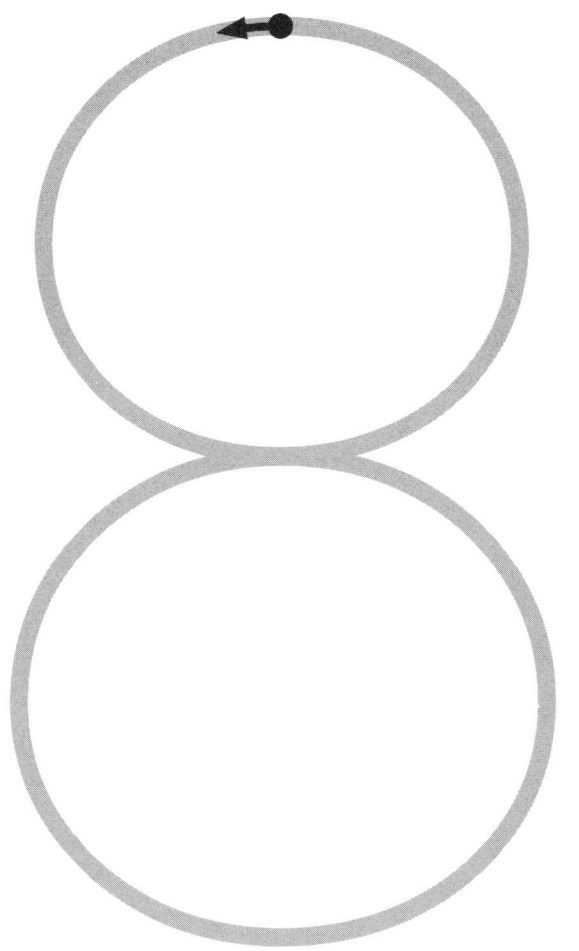

Numeracy: eight. Children say the *Number 8* Chant as they show eight fingers: *Eight, eight, show me eight. Show me eight like this.* Then, they trace the number 8. Ask: *How many flowers can you see? Let's count: one, two, three, four, five, six, seven, eight.* Repeat, encouraging children to count. Help children to count and choose eight crayons and use them to color the flowers.

Unit 8 — 113

 Say. Circle. Draw. Color.

Review

What can we see in a park?

My favorite thing in Unit 8:

Unit 8

Vocabulary and Language Review: Ask the Big Question: *What can we see in a park?* Children look back through Unit 8 to recall what they have learned. Ask them to look at the six pictures from Unit 8. They say the words and then circle the pictures that they are able to name. Then ask: *What was your favorite thing in this unit?* Remind children of the song, story, cross-curricular lesson, etc. They draw a picture of their favorite thing. Children point to and talk about their pictures. Answer the Big Question together, using their pictures as a prompt. Finally, focus on the self-assessment activity. Ask: *How did you do in this unit?* Children color the face that shows how they feel they did.

9 Where do we live?

 Point.   Stick.   Color.   Say.

Vocabulary: *city, country, house, yard.* Say each new word, and children point to each place as you say it. Say: *(House / Yard).* Stick the *(house / yard).* Children stick each sticker as you say it. Then say: *(City / Country).* Color the *city / country.* Children color each place as you say it. Finally, children point to and name each place.

◯ Circle. ◡ Say. **Story**

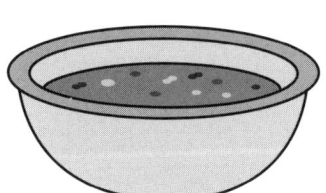

Language: *What's in the picture? There's (broth). broth, book.* Ask children to think about the story and remember what happens. Look at the first picture. Children look at each smaller picture. They circle the item that is missing from the big picture. Point to each picture and ask: *What's in the picture?* Children answer: *There's (broth).*

 Point. Say. Circle. Follow.

Phonics

Phonics: *e*lephant /e/, *o*range /ɒ/. Say the letter sounds /e/, /ɒ/. Children point to the correct letter and repeat the sounds. Next, say the words for children to point to the correct picture. Children circle the correct picture for each letter, and say the words. Finally, children follow the letters with their finger, or, if they are ready, they can trace them with a pencil.

Unit 9 117

 Look.  Match. Say.

Literacy

Literacy: Identifying the sequence of a story. Ask children to think about the story and remember what happens. Then focus on the story at the bottom of the page, and the missing pictures above it. Children look carefully and match the frames to the sequence. They then say what happens first / next / last, using the pictures as prompts.

 Draw. Say.

Values

Values: Helping at home. Point to the small pictures and ask children if they ever do each thing. Have a discussion about what things children do to help at home. Children draw themselves helping. They point and say: *I help at home.*

Unit 9

Point. Say. Draw.

Vocabulary

Vocabulary: *apartment building, window, door, street.* Children point to and name each picture. Then, they look at the pattern in each row and say what item should come next. Guide them through the first pattern. Say: *door, window, door ... What comes next? (Window.)* Children draw a window in the empty space. Continue with the other rows. Once children have finished drawing, ask them to repeat the completed patterns.

Unit 9

◯ **Circle.** ✏️ **Draw.** 😊 **Say.**

Language

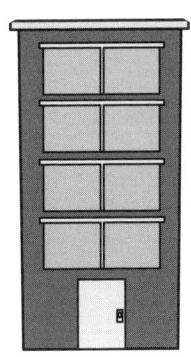

Language: *Where do you live? I live in (a house / an apartment building). Where does he / she live? He / She lives in (a house).* Ask: *Where do you live? A house or an apartment building?* Children answer. They circle the picture that shows where they live. They then draw a picture of their home. Ask individual children: *Where do you live? (I live in an apartment building.)* Finally, summarize by saying: *(Sara) lives in a house. Where does (Ali) live?* and encourage children to respond as you go around the class.

Unit 9

Concept

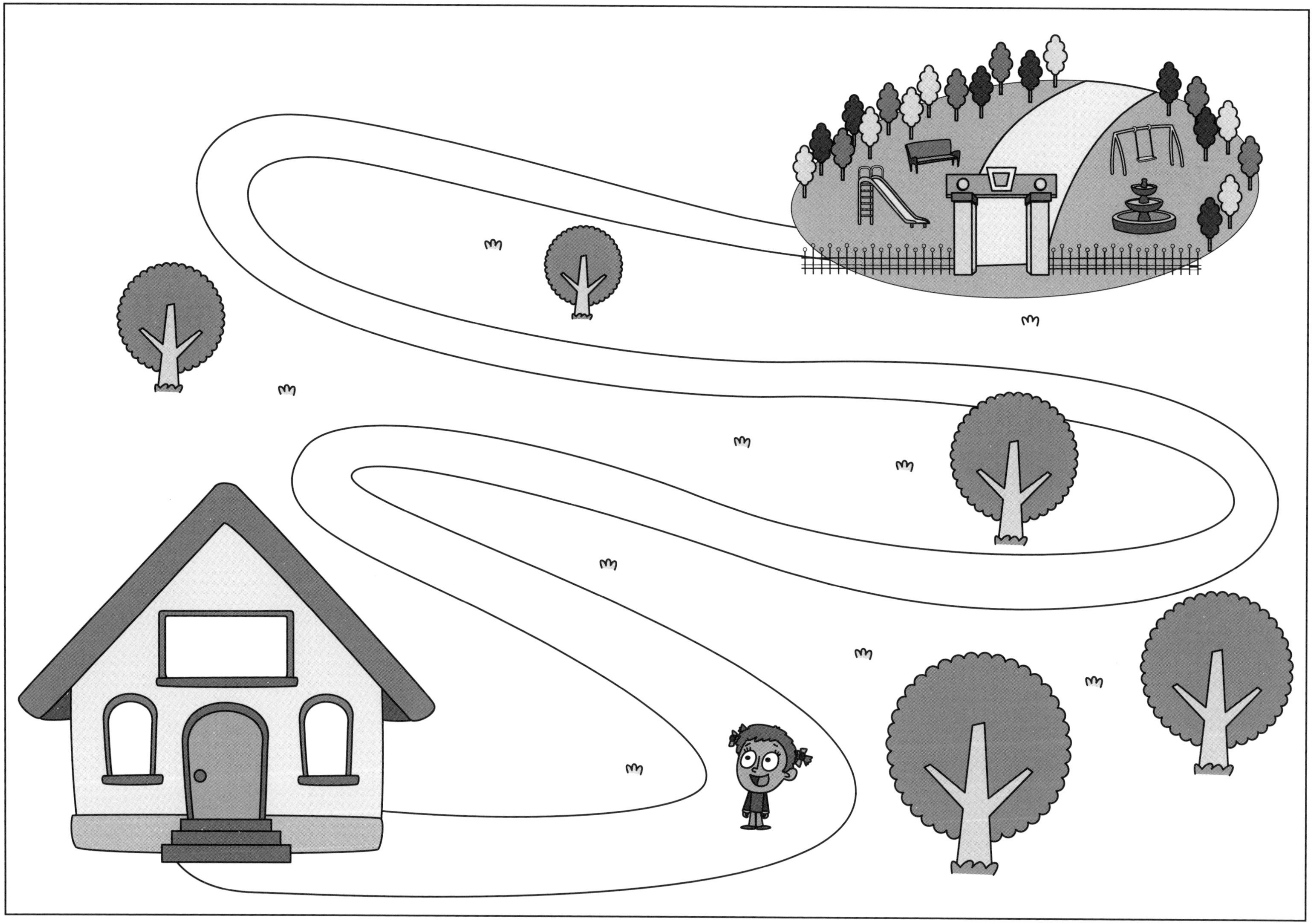

Concept: near / far. Children look at the scene and find Mia. Then say: *Point to the house. The house is near. Point to the park. The park is far.* Children draw a short line along the path from Mia to the house saying: *Near. The house is near.* They then draw a long line, following the path, from Mia to the park, saying: *Far. The park is far.*

 **Match. Say.**

Vocabulary

  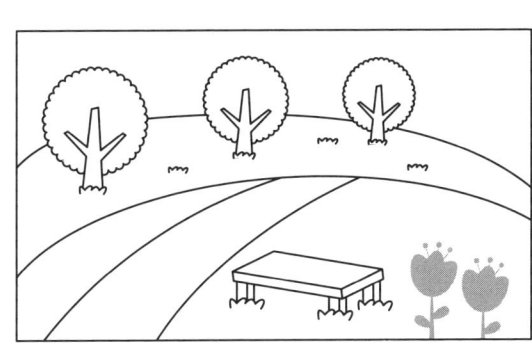 

Vocabulary: *market, toy store, park, bookstore.* Children point to and name the places on the page: *market, bookstore, park, toy store.* Then, they name the items at the top of the page: *book, flowers, teddy bear, vegetables.* They match each place to the detail that's missing from that place in the picture. Then, they say: *The (vegetables) are in the (market).*

Unit 9 123

 Circle. Say.

Language

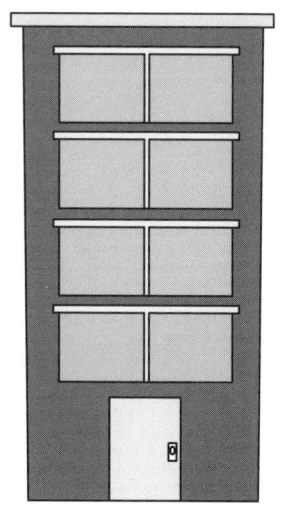

Language: *Is there a (park) near your house? Yes, there is. No, there isn't.* Children point to and name the places. Ask: *Is there a (market) near your house?* Children circle the places that are near their house. When they've finished, point to each place again and ask: *Is there a (market) near your house?* Children answer: *Yes, there is.* or *No, there isn't.*

 **Look.**  **Match.**  **Say.**

Speaking

Language: *I want to (eat an apple). Let's go to the (market)!* Look at the first picture and ask: *What does he want to do? (Eat an apple.)* Say: *I want to eat an apple. Let's go to the ...* Children say: *Market.* They find it in the town. They draw a line to match the boy to the market. Repeat with the other children and places. Finally, point to each child again and say: *I want to (eat an apple).* Children respond: *Let's go to the (market)!*

Unit 9 125

 Look. Circle.

Cross-curricular: Social Studies

Social Studies: Learning about different places. Point to the pictures at the top of each section and ask: *City or country?* Point to each item in the first section and say: *City?* Children circle the items that we see in the city. Repeat for the other section.

 Say. Trace. Count. Color. **Numeracy**

Numeracy: nine, ten. Children say the *Number 9* Chant as they show nine fingers: *Nine, nine, show me nine. Show me nine like this.* Then, they trace the number 9. Point to the number 9 and say: *What number is this? (Nine.) Let's count: One, two, three, four, five, six, even, eight, nine.* Repeat with the number 10 and the houses. Help children to count and choose nine / ten crayons and use them to color the pictures.

 Say. Circle. Draw. Color.

Review

Where do we live?

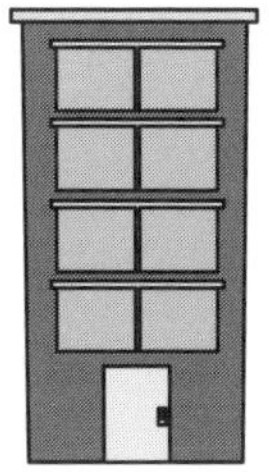

My favorite thing in Unit 9:

Unit 9

Vocabulary and Language Review: Ask the Big Question: *Where do we live?* Children look back through Unit 9 to recall what they have learned. Ask them to look at the six pictures from Unit 9. They say the words and then circle the pictures that they are able to name. Then ask: *What was your favorite thing in this unit?* Remind children of the song, story, cross-curricular lesson, etc. They draw a picture of their favorite thing. Children point to and talk about their pictures. Answer the Big Question together, using their pictures as a prompt. Finally, focus on the self-assessment activity. Ask: *How did you do in this unit?* Children color the face that shows how they feel they did.

Picture Dictionary

Children open the book to the corresponding unit. They point to a picture and name it. If children cannot name the vocabulary item, say the word and have them repeat it. Finally, children color the pictures. You can use the Picture Dictionary to review vocabulary throughout the year.

Unit 1: Vocabulary 1	Unit 1: Vocabulary 2	Unit 1: Vocabulary 3	Unit 2: Vocabulary 1
boy	book	Leo	eyes
girl	chair	Mia	face
school	crayon	Tickles	hair
teacher	table		nose

Unit 2: Vocabulary 2	Unit 2: Vocabulary 3	Unit 3: Vocabulary 1	Unit 3: Vocabulary 2
cheeks	angry	arms	elbows
ears	happy	feet	fingers
forehead	sad	hands	head
mouth		legs	knees

Unit 3: Vocabulary 3	Unit 4: Vocabulary 1	Unit 4: Vocabulary 2	Unit 4: Vocabulary 3
crawl	brother	baby	old
dance	father	grandfather	short
kick	mother	grandmother	tall
run	sister		young

Unit 5: Vocabulary 1	Unit 5: Vocabulary 2	Unit 5: Vocabulary 3	Unit 6: Vocabulary 1
bird	dog	fly	apple
cat	hamster	jump	carrot
fish	lizard	swim	pear
rabbit	turtle	walk	tomato

Unit 6: Vocabulary 2	Unit 6: Vocabulary 3	Unit 7: Vocabulary 1	Unit 7: Vocabulary 2
bananas	orange	ball	blocks
cucumbers	peas	car	kite
grapes	pineapple	doll	tricycle
lettuce	potato	teddy bear	yo-yo

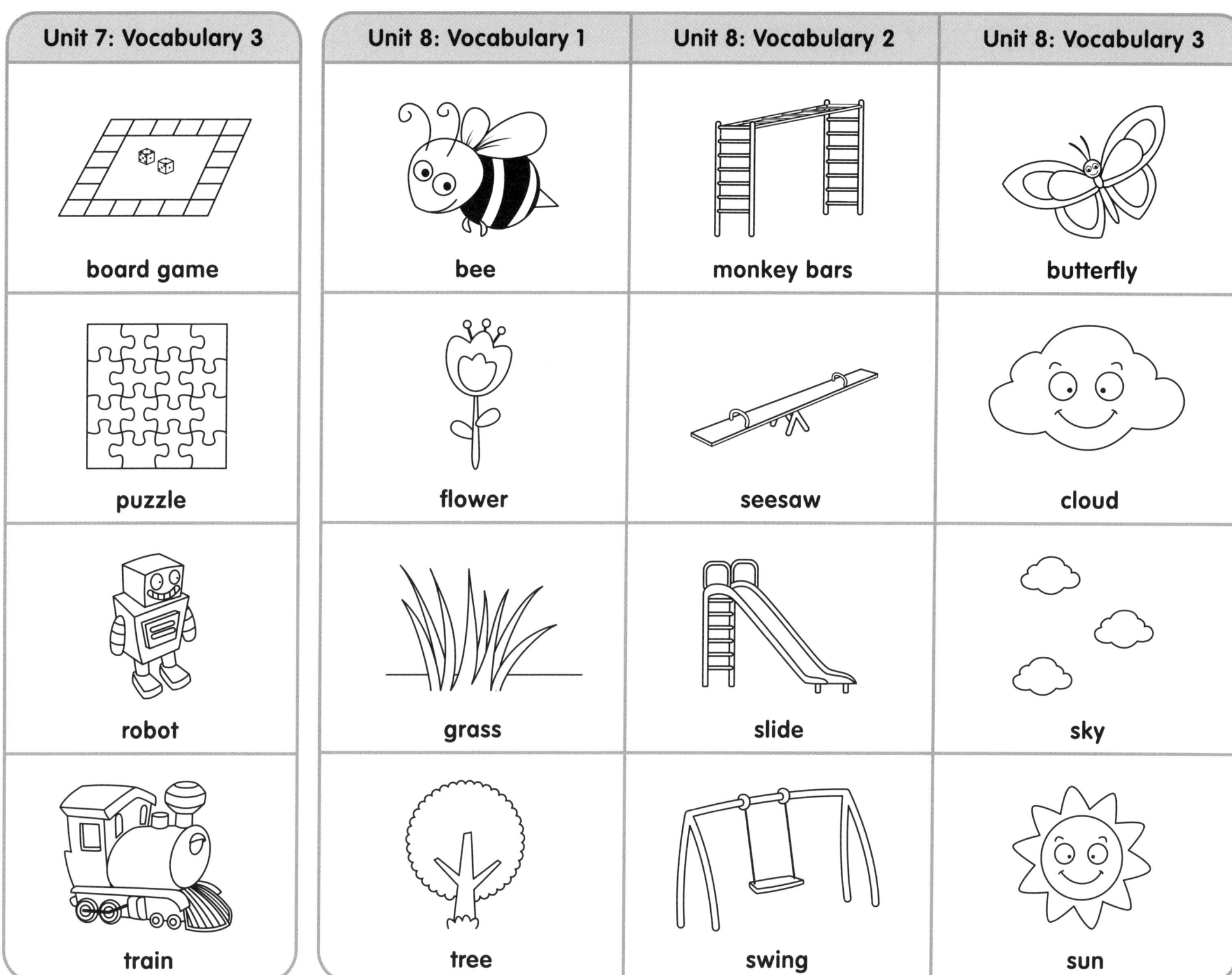

Unit 9: Vocabulary 1	Unit 9: Vocabulary 2	Unit 9: Vocabulary 3
city	apartment building	bookstore
country	door	market
house	street	park
yard	window	toy store

Unit 6, p. 73

Unit 7, p. 87

Unit 8, p. 101

Unit 9, p. 115

Unit 1, p. 3

Unit 2, p. 17

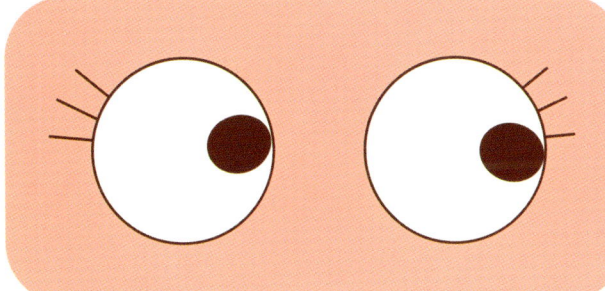 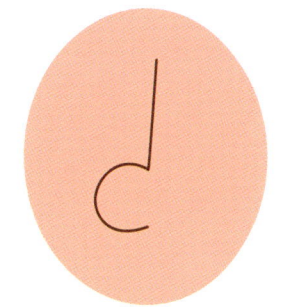

Unit 3, p. 31

Unit 4, p. 45

Unit 5, p. 59